The Language of Newspapers

Advances in Sociolinguistics
Series Editors: Professor Sally Johnson, University of Leeds
　　　　　　　Dr Tommaso M. Milani, University of the Witwatersrand

Since the emergence of sociolinguistics as a new field of enquiry in the late 1960s, research into the relationship between language and society has advanced almost beyond recognition. In particular, the past decade has witnessed the considerable influence of theories drawn from outside of sociolinguistics itself. Thus, rather than see language as a mere reflection of society, recent work has been increasingly inspired by ideas drawn from social, cultural and political theory that have emphasized the constitutive role played by language/discourse in all areas of social life. The Advances in Sociolinguistics series seeks to provide a snapshot of the current diversity of the field of sociolinguistics and the blurring of the boundaries between sociolinguistics and other domains of study concerned with the role of language in society.

Discourses of Endangerment: Ideology and Interest in the Defence of Languages
　　Edited by Alexandre Duchêne and Monica Heller

Globalization of Language and Culture in Asia
　　Edited by Viniti Vaish

Linguistic Minorities and Modernity, 2nd Edition: A Sociolinguistic Ethnography
　　Monica Heller

Language, Culture and Identity: An Ethnolinguistic Perspective
　　Philip Riley

Language Ideologies and Media Discourse: Texts, Practices, Politics
　　Edited by Sally Johnson and Tommaso M. Milani

Language in the Media: Representations, Identities, Ideologies
　　Edited by Sally Johnson and Astrid Ensslin

Language and Power: An Introduction to Institutional Discourse
　　Andrea Mayr

Language Testing, Migration and Citizenship
　　Edited by Guus Extra, Massimiliano Spotti and Piet Van Avermaet

Multilingualism: A Critical Perspective
　　Adrian Blackledge and Angela Creese

Semiotic Landscapes: Language, Image, Space
　　Adam Jaworski and Crispin Thurlow

The Languages of Global Hip-Hop
　　Edited by Marina Terkourafi

The Languages of Urban Africa
　　Edited by Fiona Mc Laughlin

The Language of Newspapers

Socio-Historical Perspectives

Martin Conboy

continuum

Continuum International Publishing Group

The Tower Building
11 York Road
London SE1 7NX

80 Maiden Lane
Suite 704
New York, NY 10038

www.continuumbooks.com

British Library Cataloguing-in-Publication Data
A catalogue record for this book is available from the British Library.

ISBN: 978-1-8470-6180-5 (Hardback)
       978-1-8470-6181-2 (Paperback)

Library of Congress Cataloging-in-Publication Data
A catalog record for this book is available from the Library of Congress.

Typeset by Newgen Imaging Systems Pvt Ltd, Chennai, India
Printed and bound in Great Britain by CPI Antony Rowe, Chippenham, Wiltshire

Contents

Acknowledgements

and how you can dispute, therefore, that a newspaper is one huge
repertory of the vices which writers should avoid, and so a widely
circulating medium of literary demoralization, I fail to see.

'Newspapers and English: A Dialogue'
Macmillan's Magazine, 1886

A book which attempts to make certain connections between the fields
of linguistics, history and journalism studies, first needs editorial
enthusiasm and support if it is ever going to emerge into the world
printed and bound or even shimmering on a screen. These were provided by Gurdeep Mattu as commissioning editor and his editorial
assistant, Colleen Coalter, at Continuum together with Sally Johnson
and later by Tommaso Milani, as series editors. In the process of bringing the manuscript to completion, Mr P. Muralidharan in Chennai
adequately demonstrated the benefits of global cooperation and proved
that geographical distance in no hindrance to courtesy. I hope the
finished product goes some way towards repaying their collective
confidence in the project.

I am grateful to Scott Dawson and Karen Lee for facilitating permis-
sion to use Gale digital archives as well as Samantha Tillett at the British
Library. Beyond the essential provision of material resources, Ed King,
Head of Collections at the British Newspaper Library, Colindale has
consistently lent his energetic support to this and all other projects,
both successful and thwarted, which attempt to shed light on the history
and fabric of newspapers.

At the University of Sheffield, the intellectual generosity and friend-
ship of John Steel and Adrian Bingham have been the chief sources of
inspiration in enabling me to work in the interdisciplinary style which
I hope is represented in the book. I am grateful to the University of
Sheffield for the generous provision of a sabbatical semester and the
leafy splendor of Nether Edge which, combined, allowed sufficient
peace and calm to complete this project. The administrative staff in the
Department of Journalism Studies especially Amanda Burton and Susie
Whitelam have continued to furnish an air of calm efficiency where
creativity has the opportunity to prosper while Alastair Allan, as our
subject specialist librarian, has championed the provision of digital

resources in the university library and has provided constant advice and strategic support.

Many colleagues past and present, too numerous to mention, may recognize shared enthusiasms and conversations in the pages of this book. My thanks to them for their patience and advice but most especially to Jane Taylor and Bob Franklin who have encouraged me simply to persevere. To all of these people, I owe a great debt of thanks which I sincerely trust is reflected in these pages. If the book falls short of its ambitions in any way then, as is customary, I must point out that it is through no shortage of support but due to the failings of the author.

Simone and Lara – Die Wilden Hühner – as always, take most credit for providing the alternative space which makes it all worthwhile and it is to them that the book is dedicated.

Introduction: The social nature of newspaper language

Structure and focus of the book

This book will deal with the very stuff of newspapers; their language. It will chart the various ways in which the shape and content of that language has impacted upon social and political debates over four centuries, from the first emergence of periodical publications in the seventeenth century to the present day. In turn, it will also assess the opposite force in this relationship; the influences of political and social changes on newspapers and how these changes have become manifest in their use of language. It hopes to be able to add a much-needed historical perspective to wider contemporary debates about the social implications of the language of the news media (Johnson and Ensslin, 2007). In doing so, it will aim to initiate a critical as well as a productive dialogue between sociolinguistics and journalism studies.

The book will highlight the ways in which newspapers have needed to accommodate social, political and technological changes throughout their history. It will take as its starting point the observation of Bell (1984: 145–204), rooted itself in sociological understanding, that journalism is an 'exercise in audience design'. This perspective emphasizes that the language of newspapers has always encapsulated what would sell to audiences and how information could best be packaged and presented to achieve this commercial end at any particular time. Newspapers have therefore always attempted to fit into the tastes of their readerships and sought ways to echo these within their own idiom, thereby reconstructing the 'original' audience in the process. Despite their underlying commercial imperative, this need to provide a distinctive language in which to give a coherent editorial expression to readers' tastes has had both conservative and radical implications at different moments in the history of the newspaper.

In structural terms, the chronology of the book will provide a long view of the changes in the language of newspapers. In doing so, it will require a certain indulgence from the reader in accepting a broad definition of newspapers to include earlier influential periodical publications which played a role in the formation of what later became identifiable as the newspaper. It will begin by considering the revolutionary implications of the first periodical publications in England and how their use of language quickly began to fuel a radically changing social and political order. This frenetic period may have come to an end with the Restoration of the monarchy in 1660 but the precedent of a regular distribution of news in print or manuscript form had been established and enabled the honing of a style of address which was suited to political and economic circumstances, as well as acceptable to a gradually broadening readership. Following a degree of political liberalization after the lapse of the Licensing Act in 1695, periodical print publications began to experiment once again with form as well as content and subsequently, the eighteenth century saw the consolidation of a bourgeois style of political engagement through the medium of periodical news production. It is this political engagement which Habermas (1992) has termed the bourgeois public sphere. Political interventions in support of popular causes effected a division between the language of the politically respectable bourgeois newspaper and that of radical periodical pamphlets in the first half of the nineteenth century which has been seen as the zenith of the influence of the 'publicists' in print (Chalaby, 1998). This was followed by a period during which newspapers learned how to make increasing profits from addressing broader social audiences in a language that matched the aspirations of those readers (Lee, 1976). The end of the nineteenth century saw the fusion, within the daily popular press in England, of certain populist techniques in newspaper language and layout, which had been developed commercially in the United States (Baldasty, 1992). These techniques, often identified as the New Journalism (Wiener, 1988), were ultimately to spread their influence throughout the entire newspaper industry.

The twentieth-century newspaper's language was shaped by a wave of technologies competing with the newspaper as the prime provider of topical information about the world. First radio, then television, satellite and most recently the internet have all forced newspapers to alter the structure and address of their language as they bid to retain a profitable and influential share of the market for news and entertainment. Out of the patterns of these media interventions over the twentieth century, one form of newspaper language has been developed to such an extent that its influence is to be observed everywhere: the tabloid. It would be no exaggeration to say that it was indeed the tabloid century, as the style of this language has had profound social and political effects upon the wider contemporary media world.

In newspapers today, we are witnessing the latest linguistic accommodation to changing social and commercial pressures. Newspapers have always striven to provide an elaborated form of conversation with their audiences, to be something more than a dry account of the events of the day. What they are now pressed to do is to provide a version of that daily conversation in an environment that has many other technologies competing to provide that sense of communal voice. The book will complete its survey by considering how newspapers of the present are dealing in their latest struggle to survive and how their language is adapting to the existence of so many other forms of contemporary communication flow. The longer historical perspective of the book will allow the reader to assess the extent to which this adaptation represents a novel departure or a reconfiguration of older social functions of their language.

Language as social activity

One of the common limitations of most books about newspapers within the tradition of media studies (Curran: 2002) is that they tend to stick to accounts of institutional and political contexts, leading them to ignore broader questions about their role as an integral part of social history. One problem associated with this approach is that newspapers are dealt with very much as commercial/political products with very little regard for the social specifics of their language. A second limitation is that by concentrating merely on the commercial or political contexts of newspapers, there is an implication that the language that they employ is a rather static commodity in the service of the dynamics of life outside their pages. Nothing could be further from the truth. In the view of this author, the language of newspapers is the most vital and dynamic aspect of their history. A third limitation is that by neglecting the importance of the language of newspapers as a significant element in their social appeal, society itself is implicitly constructed as something which sits outside language. This book would like to encourage a more energized interpretation of the relationship between language and the social audience implicit in the newspaper's text and layout. The idealized readers, constructed within the language of the newspaper, are very much part of the meaning-making process of the newspaper, as they are of news production generally (Scollon, 1998), not simply passive vessels for information.

Language is a thoroughly social activity and newspapers extend that activity beyond the confines of face-to-face discourse to an extended, imagined community of kinship based on nation (Anderson, 1986; Billig, 1995; De Cillia, Reisigl and Wodak, 1999; Conboy, 2006). Newspaper language materializes that identity quite literally onto the page. There has been a burgeoning interest in the specifics of the language of news media and its social implications (Bell, 1991; Van Dijk, 1991; Fairclough, 1995a 1995b; Conboy, 2007a; Richardson, 2007; Montgomery,

3

2007) while recent studies of the early history of newspapers have gone a long way to establishing a linguistic emphasis within studies of the emergence of periodical publications in England (Sommerville, 1996; Raymond, 1996 1999). What this project attempts to add is a bridge between the two traditions of journalism studies and discourse analysis and one which can provide a synoptic analysis of the impact of newspaper language over time. Placing language at the forefront of the study of newspapers reinforces the point that:

> . . . a concept of a language cannot stand isolated in an intellectual no-man's land. It is inevitably part of some more intricate complex of views about how certain verbal activities stand in relation to other human activities, and hence, ultimately, about man's [sic] place in society. (Harris, 1980: 54)

Accounts which downgrade the social role of language in the history of newspapers can fall into the trap which Cameron (1990) identifies as the 'language reflects society' model. She articulates the restrictions of such a view:

> The first problem is its dependence on a naïve and simplistic *social* theory . . . Secondly, there is the problem of how to *relate* the social to the linguistic (however we conceive the social). The 'language reflects society' account implies that social structures somehow exist before language, which simply 'reflects' or 'expresses' the more fundamental categories of the social . . . language . . . [is a] *part of* the social, interacting with other modes of behaviour and just as important as any of them. (Cameron, 1990: 81–82)

This restricted view is, of course, a regular cliché within lazy-minded interpretations of the role of the newspaper itself as 'mirroring society'. To counter that view, this book restores language as a centrally important social intervention to the study of the newspaper arguing with Hodge and Kress that language is:

> a key instrument in socialization, and the means whereby society forms and permeates the individual's consciousness . . . signifying social behaviour. (Hodge and Kress, 1993: 1)

Theoretical perspectives

Having asserted that we cannot consider language without its social context, it is appropriate to move on to briefly consider a range of ideas about language and society that this book will draw upon which have direct relevance to a historical study of the language of newspapers. It is to be hoped that by making explicit the theoretical claims of the argument in the early stages, the rest of the book can concentrate on providing a rich illustration of the varied language of the newspaper within that theoretical context without too much in the way of diversion. The narratives of newspapers place them unmistakenly in their times. In turn, the historical sweep and the specifics of a particular era are formative of the language of newspapers, meaning that the social character of these texts is therefore both thematic and structural. Many contemporary accounts of language and society consider that language is profoundly implicated in power structures in society (Foucault, 1974; Fairclough, 1995a 1995b; Hodge and Kress, 1993). The early destabilization of social hierarchies by periodical publications from the seventeenth century covered in this account is a first and clear testament to this, as well as being an indication of the potential for interaction between social and textual formations. Russian theorist Bakhtin (1996) provides one of the most subtle and persuasive accounts of how language is used as a key site of struggle between conflicting social forces: all of which wish to constrain meaning to their own ends and therefore give direction to communication within their own preferred definitions in order to achieve their own goals.

The key terms which we will borrow from Bakhtin are 'dialogue', and 'heteroglossia' in this introduction and 'carnivalesque' in relation to discussions of tabloid newspapers and the much contested process of 'tabloidization' flowing from these newspapers later in the book. Bakhtin's concept of heteroglossia fits well with the mapping of the history of newspaper language. It can assist in problematizing the constant power struggles over which features of newspapers have had the greatest impact on the social and political worlds at any given time and through this theoretical lens, newspaper language can be observed as a highly contested dialogic space where the struggle over hierarchies of communicative control has persisted across different historical periods.

Heteroglossia is Bakhtin's conceptualization of the fact that all language transactions take place in the context of potentially alternative expressions. They are structured between the centrifugal potential of the multiplicity of contesting voices of heteroglossia and the centripetal tendencies which allow language to retain a socially shared coherence. Heteroglossia traditionally contests the dominant social-linguistic norms. The concept foregrounds the linguistic nature of our experience of the world as it is narrated to us and through us, drawing on a vast array of voices and modes of communication, all vying in particular times and places for our attention. This has a particular relevance to the role of the newspaper which has evolved with a range of competing and overlapping functions. These include informational, political, entertainment, normative/integrationist creation of social identities, agenda-setting and consumerist all within increasingly complex networks of a more integrated and wider mediasphere. Journalism is defined in each era by its particular engagement with politics, technology, economics and culture. Dahlgren is one leading commentator who appreciates this diversity and stresses that the 'cultural discourse' (1988: 51) of journalism is not simply informational but a part of a broader set of symbolic representation. This multiplicity and generic variation has always formed part of newspaper journalism's resilience and vitality and explains much of its ability to realign within different historical and political settings (Conboy, 2004: 224).

One of the tasks of the newspaper is to close down a potentially infinite heteroglossia into a unified editorial voice but one which still may appear to draw on the energies of a multiplicity of voices and attitudes. All the newspaper's appeal as a popular product lies in its successful reconciliation between these two poles of unity and multiplicity. Within the heteroglossia of cultural discourse, however, newspapers' style and content remain determined ultimately by the voice of the political economy because they have always needed to make a profit through their selection of generic variety and political pragmatism.

Newspapers over time have adapted to articulate particular variants of language for particular social groups as Bakhtin may have envisaged. From the aspirations of the emergent bourgeoisie as a dominant economic and political grouping in the eighteenth century, articulating its new-found identity in the periodical press (Eagleton, 1991), through the era of radical engagement with political and social reform in the early nineteenth century, to the commercialization of the voice of the ordinary working classes in the *Daily Mirror* of the period 1934–1969, we can see the sort of social stratifications of language in newspaper form which had attracted the attention of Bakhtin to the work of Rabelais in a literary form at a very different historical juncture. Within their history there has been a constant struggle between differing claims on the functions and aims of newspapers. Accounts of newspapers which prioritize both their commercial concerns as well as their related reputation for scrutiny of the powerful in society (their supposed watchdog function) have predominated in historical assessments of the newspaper through history (Fox-Bourne, 1998; Siebert, 1965; Koss, 1981 and 1984) but accounts of discourses resistant to this politically conservative and economically subservient style of newspaper continue to resonate. Harrison (1974), Atton (2002) Atton and Hamilton (2008) all provide evidence of how the subordinate survives within oppositional discourses as too do the discourses of ethical journalism (Frost, 2007; Harcup, 2006) and accounts which highlight the need for journalism to survive as a counterbalance to the interests of the powerful despite the decline of the watchdog functions of journalism within the contemporary political economy of newspapers (Lewis et al., 2008a; O'Neill and O'Connor, 2008; Davies, 2008). There continues, therefore, to be a set of variable, social and political claims on the language and function of the newspaper, yet they remain constrained within a set of dominant perspectives and within historically specific social formations. This is what makes the language of newspapers such an important topic from a socio-historical point of view. It can be investigated to see how its dominant patterns fitted into or challenged social and political structures at different points in history. The proliferation of styles of newspaper language to address competing expectations and demands has complex implications:

> . . . it can be seen that the social purposes of journalism are contradictory. Some are overt (entertainment, factuality, impartiality, objectivity) some covert (social control, ideological commitment, legitimation) and the overt and the covert purposes do not mesh easily. It is perhaps not surprising that in a situation of such contradictory generic demands a rich array of generic strategies has developed. (Van Leeuwen, 1987: 209)

The issue of genre has particular importance for this study since, as well as having stylistic characteristics, genre is also a form of social contract between writer and reader. A reader knows what to expect from a particular genre or combination of genres (Swales, 1990) and takes his/her place in the strategic social complexity of these expectations (Fairclough, 2005: 71). These expectations form part of a shared sense of community in reading and are an important contributor to the social aspects of writing. Generic patterns and the expectations of readers of newspapers have always been conditioned within such social parameters. Miller (1994) argues that genre functions as a way of understanding how to participate in the activities of a community. As such, genre is located within a wider set of cultural patterns and in studying the particular features of these patterns over time we can begin to understand more about the ways in which readers shared their social knowledge. Newspaper language can be seen very much as a 'social semiotic' (Halliday, 1978) which, in its generic range, draws particular social groups into particular styles of presentation.

Newspapers have always created readers, not news, as their primary function. They are 'language forming institutions' (Bell, 1991: 7), informing as well as responding to broader linguistic trends and contributing to the 'emergent property of social interaction' (Pennycook, 2004: 7). Yet, even within the informational function of the newspaper, there have always been ideological implications in the transmission of information for particular audiences. Newspapers function to create public identities for social groups as well as for individuals within those groups though the range of textual strategies identified by Fairclough (2003: 213–221). This view of the language of newspapers complements the 'ritual view of communication' espoused by Carey (1989) who argued that the media, and for our purposes this can be applied to the more specific medium of the newspaper, are far more concerned with the re-creation and reconfirmation of social groups than they are with the transmission of information *per se*. Language is a fundamental aspect of this ritualization, each group recognizing its own vernacular and each newspaper trying its best to maintain a particular brand of language to hold together its own social, geographical, demographic and political readership.

Another perspective from linguistics which can be deployed to understand the social history of the language of the newspaper comes from Ferdinand de Saussure (1966). Semiology encourages us to create a distance from the everyday routines of linguistic performance, to see language in a denaturalized way. It does this by creating a series of binary oppositions some of which have implications for our study of the language of the news media. One of the most useful of these for our analytical purposes is that of *langue/parole*. For de Saussure, *langue* [the structure of language] and *parole* [the more malleable performance of everyday speech] play an essential role in the function of language. These poles have a special relevance to the language of newspapers. *Langue* can be interpreted as the systematic structuring of language as news within institutional norms of news value (Harcup and O'Neill, 2001) or house style (Cameron, 1996); *parole* as the vernacular echoes of a socially targeted, idealized audience. This binary dynamic is a point which is endorsed in the interplay between the individual and the institutional in the interpretation of journalism by Bourdieu: '. . . even if the actors have an effect as individuals, it is the *structure* of the journalistic field that determines the intensity and orientation of its mechanisms, as well as their effects on other fields' (Bourdieu, 1998: 73). Although he was thinking more of the journalist as actor rather than the reader at this point of his argument, the oppositional dynamic between individual and structure and the effect of this dynamic on the production of the newspaper's language remains valid. Newspapers have always provided a constant negotiation between these perspectives as they attempt to maintain a grip on that language of the quotidian par excellence, the news. Moreover, the 'essential relatedness of language and history' (Crowley, 1990: 29–37) is clarified according to Crowley through de Saussure's analytical framing, ensuring that the relationship is not an 'external' factor to the main business of linguistic study.

This inter-relatedness explains how a relatively stable worldview retains coherence for an audience over time. Newspaper language can only function in a way which accepts the historical rooting of that language as an essential part of its context. An obvious example would be the way that the anniversaries of war are commemorated, where the past is the central point of the contemporary story (Conboy, 2007a) and where the reader is expected to make the connection for themselves from within the accepted cultural framework of the newspaper's language (Conboy, 2007a: 97).

A first definition of discourse is in terms of the coexistence of text and context and the impossibility of understanding one without the other or prioritizing one as more important than the other. Both text and context are complex, as is their inter-relationship. Broadly speaking, linguists choose to use the term discourse as describing the coexistence of text and context, and the regularities present in any stretch of language longer than a sentence (Crystal, 1991: 106). This implies that there can be, from the perspective of a discursive analysis, no utterance which can be divorced from the circumstances of its production and reception, beyond the utterance itself in its interconnections with other linguistic and non-linguistic phenomena, without losing an essential part of its meaning: its context. The relevance of this to the language of newspaper journalism is clear. It means that we must always keep in mind the multiple relationships of journalism with society, within the economy, with politics and also as a relatively autonomous cultural practice in its own right with its own traditions. Journalism can be viewed as an intersection of many conflicting interests, some of which, at some points in history, have clearer priority than others.

Discourse, in the second sense in which it is often used in contemporary debates around language and culture, is a term influenced by the writing of Michel Foucault (1974). This definition too has a direct relevance to newspapers as it is predominantly concerned with the social function of language. This view of discourse claims that the language used about a particular practice in turn constructs the object of which it speaks meaning that this journalistic medium is therefore made up of the claims and counter-claims of a variety of speakers on its behalf. What journalists say about their work, what critics and political commentators say about journalism, the perceived effects of the language of journalism on society, the patterns of popularity among readers and viewers of journalism all take their place in defining the discourse of journalism. Discourses, according to Foucault, are also intrinsically bound up with questions of power since they give expression to the meanings and values of institutions or practices and, in doing so, claim authority for themselves. The discourse of journalism defines, describes and limits what it is possible to say with respect to journalism, whether at its margins or at its institutional core. It describes the ways in which it is possible to think about and criticize the characteristic practices of journalism. One advantage of considering journalism in this way is to once again denaturalize certain common-sense assumptions made about it and enable us to criticize them and question their logic. Furthermore, this approach also assists in assessing how the dominant opinions in debates over journalism's power and value have altered over time. Certainly, over time, many aspects of journalism can be regarded discursively such as the freedom of the press, the news media as a 'Fourth Estate', the objectivity of journalism, the normative political functions of journalism or what journalism should and should not do and the often obscured economic imperative of journalism – its political economy.

Another advantage of considering newspaper language as a discourse is that it enables us to view news production and dissemination as creating new forms of power as well as new forms of access to representation. Journalism has never simply contested a sort of political power which lay outside its own sphere of influence. It has always been deeply involved in the creation of power structures – particularly those involved in public communication. One of the most widespread fallacies, the Whig account of journalism (cf Curran and Seaton, 2003) sees journalism as the triumphant march of the political emancipation of Western societies as enacted through the news media (Siebert, 1965). Journalism has contributed itself to this account and draws upon it as a way of legitimating its relationship with the political status quo. Considering journalism as a discourse disrupts this account and highlights its contested nature as well as encouraging us to see it as the sum of the variety of practices which it has incorporated over the centuries. Much of journalism's resilience and vitality come, in fact, from its ability to adapt to changes in cultural and economic imperatives. Writing specifically about newspapers, Black sees their history as being profoundly informed by the changes necessary within a competitive market:

> Change is therefore a central theme in newspaper history, not only because of its occurrence, and the speed of its occurrence, but also as the awareness of change creates a sense of transience and opportunity. Each period of English newspaper history can be presented as one of transformation, shifts in content, production, distribution, the nature of competition, and the social context. (Black, 2001: 1)

Foucault's view of language as playing a central role in maintaining social control and delimiting social and political change through the

10

operation of discourse is one which has been influential in developing theories of critical discourse analysis which have been applied to newspaper language most notably by (Fowler, 1991; Van Dijk, 1991; Wodak, 2001; Jäger, 2001; Cameron, 1996; Billig, 1995; Fairclough, 1995 a and b and 2003). Within this discursive environment, readers can be 'manipulated and informed, preferably manipulated while they suppose they are being informed' (Hodge and Kress, 1993: 6). Voluntarist and institutionalist concepts of language (Joseph and Taylor, 1990: 11) are involved in the power struggle over the identity of newspaper discourse since it invites deliberation on whether it is constructed predominantly by individuals (printers, politically engaged citizens, royalty, political authority) or by an institutionalized set of norms which act, even at the birth of the newspaper acted to constrain in order to meet social and political expectations. The struggle over the resolution of these questions is what forms the discourse of the newspaper. What Said has expressed more generally in connection with writing has resonance for the formation of the discourse of the newspaper more specifically:

> writing is no private exercise of a free scriptive will but rather the activation of an immensely complex tissue of forces for which a text is a place among other places where the strategies of control in society are conducted. (Said, 1978: 673–714)

Historical perspectives on the operation of these discourses through the language of newspapers can demonstrate how these are not static but attempt to manoeuvre to maintain maximum control in changing political and economic circumstances. This approach is, in fact, most productive when considering the shifts in newspaper language over time and the social and political implications of these shifts (Jucker, 2005).

Conclusion

The book will provide an outline of the changes in the language of newspapers in the context of the sociolinguistic debates briefly sketched above and the importance of those changes to the societies they were produced for and which they structured in the process of reporting them. Changes in language/format could be prompted by political changes in control or in experimentation due to a weakening of direct control; they could also be triggered by the need to differentiate for particular markets or to accommodate changes in technology. Particular phases of the development of the language of newspapers have encompassed particular engagements between language and the social and political structures dominant at those times. The book will endeavour to demonstrate how certain developments took place in negotiation with broader factors. These developments will be illustrated by examples from newspapers at key moments. At times, the interests of newspaper language were in keeping with the political ambitions of leading groups; at other times it was in conflict with them; at others, it was a commercially pragmatic compromise between the needs of readers and the needs of owners and politicians. What we are left with is often a classic Gramscian hegemonic settlement, where the acquisition of power depends as much on the consent or resignation of those disenfranchised as it does upon the might of those with the instruments of communicative authority at their disposal and where this consent is threaded through with the subtle workings of ideology, defined as a form of political common sense. The discursive interpretation of hegemony articulated by Laclau and Mouffe (1985) has particular relevance for the interpretation of newspaper language as a site of struggle over competing social and political views of the power of readers as informed citizens. While we are often presented with accounts of the history of newspapers in terms of claims to 'freedom of speech', 'objectivity', 'impartiality' and the 'public interest', these are already deeply embedded in the particular discursive parameters which have been negotiated between polity and economic structures over time. Readerships, new technologies, politicians, journalists themselves all are capable of significantly altering the discourse of newspapers and their language has had to accommodate aspects of all of them. At particular junctures in the history of the newspaper, there have been moments of discursive realignment, by which we mean in Foucault's terms, when there are changes in what newspapers as an institution can say and what they are prevented from saying, implicitly or explicitly, if they wish to maintain their authority and control over issues of knowledge and power: issues which have always been fundamental to their credibility. This credibility is always bound up with how they communicate to socially situated readers both across time, maintaining their identity, and within specific historical moments, or diachronically and synchronically in de Saussure's terms. These junctures can often shift the emphasis from language to the area of ethics or professionalism but the debate remains one predominantly about language and indeed about the generic range of language which can potentially claim the communicative space of the newspaper. This book is a brief account of some of the sociolinguistic shifts in that set of relationships.

1 Society writes back

Introduction

There had already been a range of outlets for the dissemination of topical information before the introduction of printing to Western Europe in the middle of the fifteenth century, but these had most often involved a great deal of centralized control – political or ecclesiastical – and took the form of proclamations, sacred manuscripts, edicts or formal announcements of state decisions. To these we can add the informal commentary and dissemination of the ballad. The former depended on handwritten manuscripts, the latter on traditions of oral transmission. As commodity capital established itself in the Early Modern period, possession of extensive information about events in the contemporary world was as much a matter of social status as it was of political or economic survival (Briggs and Burke, 2002) and consequently, printing enabled an increased flow of both official and unofficial news in various forms. Both began a loosening up of the social networks of communication by increasing the number and range of voices in circulation. Newsletter writers had started to develop a structured form of information distribution following on from the kind perfected by the Fuggers, a powerful banking family in Central Europe in the mid-fifteenth century, who employed a chain of well-placed informants to provide them with the latest news pertaining to their business and political interests from around their trading areas of Western Europe and the Middle East. The application of the new technology of printing to the dissemination of news not only inverted social hierarchies of control over communication by allowing the commercial consideration of the printers to challenge the political considerations of ruling elites, but it also began a process of blending the careful textual construction of the newsletter scribes with the popular appeal which had characterized oral literature. The language of printed news material, even before the advent of formal periodical newsbooks and newspapers, was involved in a dialogic exchange with non-literate culture; printed works being disseminated by word of mouth, transforming the culture of the 'illiterate', and the oral modes of communication shaping the structure of printed works (Watt, 1991; Ong, 1982). This meant that printed news could gradually begin to combine both social and aesthetic aspects in its presentation, which would hold out the promise of a widening audience and an attractive potential for profit for those able to harness this twin appeal. The aesthetic attraction of news as an activity with its own integrity has also been noted:

> News was supposed to be consumed not only because it enabled social exchange, or facilitated rational behaviour, but as an end in itself. (Raymond, 1996: 2)

The social challenge of news

The regular circulation of news in printed form implied, through its style and address, that it was intended for an audience that was significantly wider than traditional social and religious elites. This enhances the relevance to this account of contemporary analysts' views of language as a 'social semiotic' (Halliday, 1978) since the communicative form of printed news told the audience not only about the state of the world in provisional form but also about their status as recipients of this news. In addition, it allowed a dawning realization of the implications of the changing social composition of a world which was structured increasingly by an understanding of current affairs which could be gleaned on a regular basis for a modest financial outlay. What energized this social form of communication still more was the fact that it could be sold as a commodity, for profit, so that broadening the base of news consumers, through style and popular appeal, meant printers making more money.

The original news genre was the narrative report and it developed within a specific set of socio-historical processes. News, as Sommerville (1996) has indicated, formed part of a radical break in the epistemology of Western Europe and it acted as a challenge to customary political restrictions on the flow of information at the same time as its language experimented with styles which could appeal to a wider social market. Thus, from the first, printed news was generically associated with social expectations (Swales, 1990) which placed printed news within a political framework which ensured that the advent of printed news was accompanied both by sets of restrictions as well as accommodations with the structures of political control (Siebert, 1965) which allowed the Tudor monarchs to work within their own political and religious desiderata:

> Tudor monarchs, regardless of their religious allegiances, recognized the printed word's potential power to achieve their religious, political, and cultural ends. In this respect they employed their

prerogative to grant both authority and economic benefits to the printers. (Clegg, 1997: 24)

Even a publishing industry under the strict control imposed by the Tudors was problematic for the state, for often it was the scurrilous, the dangerous, the unlicensed information which the public was most eager to read. Topical versions of political affairs and religious tracts found themselves in company with more sensational fare such as reports of local fires and murders, often in the form of ballads. Published material had, prior to printing, drawn upon much longer cultural and political narratives which relied upon the authority of the Church and the related divine power of the monarch whereas the mechanical reproduction of printed news created a language which could shape discussions of contemporary political and social affairs:

> Over the course of the seventeenth century, the news had also generated an extended present of duration, not instant. Or, to put it another way, it had carved out a 'detemporalized zone' between past and future, a zone that offered a space for the discussion of current events . . . (Woolf, 2001: 109)

Bourdieu (1998) has written of the importance of understanding the range of social and political networks which culminate in what he has called the 'journalistic field'. In the early decades of periodical printed news, the social and political expectations of a particular class of news reader broadened out in ways which began to shift the existing parameters of social experience and the literate subject's 'habitus' became diversified to encompass a novel range of structural approaches to the representation of the contemporary world. This discourse of early printed news had to fit pragmatically within dominant political and economic models yet was able to shift and test the boundaries of what was permitted as the demands and expectations of its consumers changed.

The prehistory of newspapers

Caxton had introduced his Westminster Press in 1476 and by the early sixteenth century, news pamphlets were first appearing. The earliest example in English is the 1513 account of the Battle of Flodden; *hereafter ensue the trewe encounter or batayle lately done between Englande and Scotlande*. This outlined the progress of the English king and his army to the north, the strategies of battle, impressions of the conduct of the rival armies and the eventual outcome, including casualties and a list of knighthoods awarded to the English military leaders. It also contains a woodcut illustrating preparations for the battle. This news was also distributed simultaneously in ballad form under the title of 'A Ballad of the Scottyshe Kynge'.

Printed accounts of the past and present achievements of the Kings of England were often government publications and were presented in formal language to an audience presumed passive to the influence of the information. There was no assumption made in the text that these communications were a source of debate or invited involvement of any sort by the populace. They were strictly for information only. A good example is William Rastell's 420 page account of the reign of Henry VII, published under the title *Fabyans Chronycle* in 1533: 'newly printed with the cronycle, actes, and dedes done in the time of the most excellent prynce kynge Henry the vii . . .'

It was not until the accession of Henry VIII that the social and political impact of print was beginning to be appreciated as its use spread from arts and literature to the political and religious controversies of the day. Henry VIII's reforms were widely publicized during the Reformation in the form of news pamphlets printed by those eager to make a profit out of it. Although the 1534 Act of Supremacy meant that the monarch had total control of the state, church and naturally printing, in the first half of the sixteenth century, the English gentry was coming to realize that, in the Europe of the Renaissance, education was becoming essential to maintain traditional patterns of power and the grammar schools, founded for the purpose of educating their sons, were able to use the printed material provided by the expanding printing industry. At the same time, the vernacular-based teachings of the Reformation saw the rapid rise of a literate clergy and congregations more inclined to turn to English translations of sacred texts. In this way the ground was prepared for a loosened relationship between older traditions of authority and the printed word (Levy, 11–13). However, when opinion on political conjecture was printed, it could bring the full power of the state down on the author. In 1579, John Stubbe wrote a significant 44 page pamphlet in reaction to speculation that Elizabeth had offered herself in marriage to the duc d'Anjou, the brother of the King of France, Henry III, in order to delay the annexation of the Netherlands by Spain:

> The Discourie of a Gaping Gulf Whereinto England is like to be swallowed by another French marriage; if the Lord forbid not the banes, by letting her Maiestie see the sin and punishment thereof.

The pamphlet presumed to alert readers to the dangers to the monarch and her country in this course of action, concluding in the following terms:

> . . . we cannot chuse but . . . conclude that thys French marriage, is the straightest line that can be drawn fro Rome to the utter ruine of

> our church: & the very rightest perpendicular downfall that can be
> imagined fro the point France to our English state . . .

Stubb was tried and imprisoned but despite the Queen's desire that he
should be executed for this 'lewde and seditious book' his punishment
was reduced to having his right hand severed.

War provided an immediate best-selling topic for publication. It could
be embroidered by dramatizing the very process of newsgathering itself
which could be particularly striking at a time when the logistics of commercial information gathering and publication were a communicative
novelty. *News from Antwerp* (1580) added a frisson of espionage and
treachery by claiming that the letters drawn upon for its account had
been intercepted from the hands of spies and that they proved the
impossibility of negotiating a lasting peace with a treacherous Spain:

> A speciall view of the present affayres of the lowe Countreyes:
> Revealed and brought to light, by sundrie late intercepted Letters, of
> certain vizarded and counterfeit Countrymen of the same Countreys.

England's involvement in the war against Philip II first stimulated
a regular English interest in printed news which materialized in a
marked increase in the numbers of news pamphlets in the 1590s (Voss,
2001). Their primary purpose was propaganda in the service of building
a national consensus around the heroism of the English forces overseas.
In addition, it was a good way for the authorities to set the record straight,
as rumour and disinformation circulated quite freely among court as
well as around the country. The acquisition of colonies and the rise of
England as a maritime power after the victory over the Spanish Armada
in 1588 led to an increase in commodity wealth in England and a corresponding rise of a commercial class to rival the landed aristocracy. So it
is no surprise that the most famous intelligence gatherer of this era, John
Chamberlain, began his work in 1588 as news became increasingly
traded as a commodity in lubrication of other commodities.

John Wolfe, a printer and publisher, was recruited by Lord Burghley,
the Principal Minister of the Queen to distribute translations of Protestant propaganda to Catholic countries such as France and Italy. He also
developed the first corantos translated into English and experimented
with the compilation of news pamphlets in a series but as yet one lacking in regularity of publication. *Credible Reportes from France, and
Flanders. In the moneth of May. 1590* gives an illustration of the style
of these early narrative reports:

> A weeke since, came from Diepe a certaine Bark the which arrived
> at Plymouth which reported, that the governor of Diepe, was come
> to Diep after the battaile sicke of an ague, and that during his

> sicknes, the Papistes murmured, and woulde not suffer the exercise
> of Religion . . . The Governour of Renes hath cuased one friar to be
> hanged, and half a dosen of the Chiefest of the Citty, who did call
> the King hereticke.

In contrast, there was still no appetite among the political elite for any
wider dissemination of parliamentary news. For instance, Siebert
records that in 1589 the discussion of Parliamentary matters among out-
siders prompted the Speaker to reprimand the members of the House:

> that Speeches used in this House by the Members of the same be not
> any of them made or used as Table-talk, or in any wise delivered in
> notes of writing to any person or persons whatsoever not being
> Members of this House. (Siebert, 1965: 103)

However, an arresting example of the new range of language afforded
to political debate in print is provided by the appearance between
October 1588 and September 1589 of the Martin Marprelate tracts.
Evading government press controls and the vested interests of the printing establishment, a secret movable printing press was deployed to
disseminate seven satirical tracts by radical, puritan reformers against
the authority of church and state. They were used to spread radical,
religious opinion as well as to entertain in satirical fashion and drew in
a larger readership for these discussions through their use of a popular
polemic. The first tract, an epistle *To the right puissant and terrible
Priests, my clergie masters of the Confention house* was published in
1588 and itemizes the sins of its targets among the church hierarchy:

> And take heed brethren of your reverend and learned brother
> Martin Marprelate. For he meaneth in these reasons following I can
> tell you, to prove that you ought not to be maintained by the author-
> itie of the Magistrate in any Christian commonwealth: Martin is a
> shrewd fellow, and reasoneth thus. Those that are pettie popes and
> pettie Antichrists, ought not to be maintained in any Christian com-
> monwealth. But every Lord Bishop in England are pettie popes and
> pettie Antichrists . . . our Prelates usurp their authoritie
> . . . Helpe the poore people to the meanes of their salvation, that
> perish in their ignorance: make restitution unto your tenants and
> such as from whome you have wrongfully extorted anything: usurpe
> no longer, the authoritie of making of ministers and excommunica-
> tion: Let poore men be no more molested in your ungodly courts . . .
> Take no more bribes . . . All in a word, become good Christians.

The Marprelate attacks on clerics were highly personalized and provided a foretaste of how similar invective could be put to political
purposes in the English Civil War. In fact, by naming the bishops and
their victims, the author lends considerable credibility to his claims to

dealing with 'matters of fact' (Clegg, 1997: 189) as part of a cultural shift towards the generic expectations of news as commentary and polemic on contemporary affairs. Furthermore, it confirmed the potential of printed material to push forward demands for an increased pace of religious reform which aligned with the views of many within the Puritan-dominated printing community. Moreover, in their combination of insolence towards authority and the claims they made to be based in corroborated fact, the tracts also demonstrated the potential for print to challenge the basis for social consensus. It was the very language of these tracts and not just their argumentative and oppositional stance which constituted such a dynamic innovation:

> By attacking the bishops in language hitherto used only for the personal, Martin Marprelate decoupled the decorum of language from the decorum of subject. (Levy, 1999: 33)

Newsletter writers: A new class of reader

The late sixteenth century saw an increase in the London trade in news pamphlets dealing in the relatively uncontentious; sensationalist news of murders, witchcraft and strange apparitions. The Court, the Inns of Law, and the lanes around St Paul's became in Elizabethan times a network of gossip and here news was disseminated through the means of the newsletter. The newsletters offered a varied diet, including political and social news of the court but also details of trials and a smattering of strange happenings and gossip from home and abroad. They were also more expensive and therefore more restricted in distribution than the printed newsbooks which followed. In comparison with printed newsbooks, they were a more intimate medium and less likely to be read aloud to groups or to be sold on second-hand at a reduced price like the newsbooks. Newsletters came to combine both handwritten and printed material. They could include among other things: 'corantos, proclamations, copies of letters, death notices, verses, extracts from banned books, pamphlets and foreign newspapers . . .' (Atherton, 1999: 52–53). The newsletters were important not only for the information they contained but in the way their compilers were able to use them to establish and structure the network of contacts they had built up in the pursuit of their trade. These networks would come to provide the information sources for more regular printed publications. 'Intelligencers' gathered information from their sources around the nodes of power in London, much of which was gathered from personal conversations or reports of such conversations and distributed it on a regular basis in the form of letters to their powerful patrons. What had started as a personalized correspondence became a professional service which could provide a lucrative living for somebody with a network of informants, credibility among a wide range of clients wealthy enough to invest in such a bespoke service and the ability to synthesize the information in an accessible style within a short period of time. The style of the letters was by necessity deferential as they were written to high ranking public figures by more lowly informants. This implied that they did not presume to guide the reader by suggestions of opinion or emphasis. These letters were copied on behalf of the information gatherers by scriveners. These semi-professional newswriters had a reputation for accurate reporting to uphold in order to maintain the credibility of their sources and the reliability of their work and to distance their material from the embroidery to be found in the circulation of popular news in the ballad form.

The common perception among critics, however, was that news was untrustworthy, prone to exaggeration and that its dependence on novelty for its profits even provided a rationalization for deliberate invention and deceit. Woolf explains that the distrust of the new genre of printed news emanated from problems in verifying what it claimed and the general lack of authority that surrounded anything other than texts which were supported by the authority of tradition (2001: 101). In fact, there was much talk and writing of the spread of news in medical terms as if it was a disease or an 'itch' in the seventeenth century (Atherton, 1999). There was also a class perspective in these criticisms of printed news since those from elite circles were able to read and contribute to manuscript newsletters of their own and as they knew their sources, more often than not, they were therefore not dependent on the widely circulated commodity news intended for those lower down the social scale:

> . . . the news had spread to the vulgar. Matters of state, once the *arcana imperii* restricted to those fitted by birth and education to a wise understanding of their intricacies, had become the common discourse of the masses. (Atherton, 1999: 56)

In 1620 Ben Jonson wrote a court entertainment called *News from the New World* which mocked the new craze for information from very much the perspective that it breached the communicative privileges of the nobility. Later, in 1626, he presented these ideas in the form of a play, *The Staple of News*, which depicted with, 'dripping scorn, a syndicate of newsmongers bent on achieving a monopoly over the distribution of fresh intelligence' (Sherman, 2001: 24). In the opening act, a dialogue outlines an awareness that news was tailored to suit the needs of its commercial audience with all the implications he claims this held for reliability. 'News by the alphabet' is subdivided into 'authentical' and 'apocryphal', 'news of doubtful credit', 'news of the season', 'Protestant news', 'pontifical news' and one character protests:

> Why, methinks, sir, if the honest common people
> Will be abused, why should not they have their pleasure
> In the believing lies are made for them . . . (Cunningham, 1816: 285–286)

Richard Brathwaite in his *Whimzies: Or a New Cast of Characters* (1631) provides an early sceptical set of observations on how news writers used their language to lure their readers into the cycle of periodicity and to 'delude the vulgar' (Brathwaite: 21). The corano-coiner is described in the same document as the balladeer and the almanac-maker, demonstrating the simultaneity of many concerns around the dissemination of topical information in print. Of the coranto-coiner he writes,

> He retaines some militarie words of art, which hee shootes at random: no matter where they hit, they cannot wound any. He ever leaves some passages doubtfull, as if they were some more intimate secrecies of State, clozing his sentence abruptly – *With heerafter you shall heare more*. Which words, I conceive, hee onely useth as baites, to make the appetite of the Reader more eager for the next week's pursuit for a more satisfying labour. Some generall-erring relations he picks up, as Crummes or fragments, from a frequented *Ordinario*: Of which shreads he shapes a Cote to fit any credulous foole that will weare it. (Brathwaite, 1631: 16)

Corantos: Early commercialization of news

The outbreak of the Thirty Years' War in 1620 provided the political trigger for the emergence of periodical news in England. There were several different levels of national interest in the process of the war. James' daughter Princess Elizabeth had married Frederick, Elector of the Palatinate who had subsequently accepted the crown of Bohemia against the wishes of the Holy Roman Emperor. Many wanted an intervention on behalf of the Protestant forces because there were rising fears about the future of reformed religion in England. English mercenaries and money were also involved in the growing conflict, adding still more newsworthiness to events. To pander to these various interests and the reasonable desire of printers to make money out of the public's curiosity, in 1621 the government allowed the printing of corantos in English in London. At first they appeared irregularly but their printers soon realized that numbering promoted expectation and recall by readers which would boost regular habits of readership and early editors such as Thomas Gainsford, from 1622, were employed to provide more flowing narratives and continuities between editions.

The corantos generally avoided controversial aspects of domestic politics in case their printers lost their lucrative licenses or suffered more draconian prosecution. Nevertheless, material printed in the United Provinces or the German states and then imported, provided enough controversial material to keep the corantos interesting for readers. Material which was too controversial, such as accounts of parliamentary discussions, could always be included as 'separates' within newsletters. It was the 'separate', for instance, which provided the first printed account of the proceedings of Parliament in 1628. However, the level of censorship does not explain by itself the lack of home news. In general terms, news from home was less interesting because it was more generally available through personal contacts and less of an attractive and exotic commodity. In addition, foreign news was implicitly critical of James I's foreign policy by its very existence (Baron, 2001: 44) and had the added attraction for publishers, that such news tended, especially the religious variety from Europe, to be more sensational and gruesome – even with more scope for embroidery. There was more evidence in the reports from foreign wars that the great apocalyptic battle between the forces of good and evil was being enacted which many believed was an indicator of the imminence of Christ's return to earth and judgement day.

Here we have several brief examples from issue 14 of *The Affaires and Generall Businesse of Europe* more particularly (24 February 1624). The sequencing was already an indicator of an important innovation of these periodicals. Dating and sequencing structured their publication in the expectation that more would follow on particular topics and identifiable stories.

> Severall Ambassadors at Rome
>   The King of Congo in Aethiopia hath sent to Rome for Priests to be instructed in true Religion; for they are willing to forsake their Idols.

This was continued as a narrative strand in issue number 16, which announced:

> The sending of Friers from the Pope to Congos, King in Aethiopia.

There are early experiments in this same issue with headlines to indicate stories covered, a running order and an indication of the weaving of popular and political even at this early stage.

> Two Wonderful and Lamentable accidents herein related; the one shewing the great losse and fearfull shipwracke caused by the last tempest, with the fight betweene those *Dunkerkers* and the

Hollanders, which hath so long continued *in our coast in the* Downes, *of whom some escaped, some were sunke, the rest staid.*

The other of a maiden who through her extreme pride was personally deceived by the Devill, who afterwards ended her life most miserably. (October 11)

In the same issue, great store is set in the specific approach to the reader; it starts, 'Gentle Reader' and by frequent mentions of 'we', emphasizing the idea that the coranto could be a communal activity involving, just as newsletters, communication among a network of committed participants. The explicit process of weaving letters received into an informed commentary on foreign, political and military affairs in an early example of editorial work informs an assumed readership of the political contexts of information just as the more personalized newsletters would have done.

> *From Venice the tenth of February*
> The Letters from *Venice* are of divers sorts; for they intreat of sundry matters; but the principal abstracts may be thus set down . . .'
> The last letter we have received from *Venice* saies plainly, that there is great preparation made in Spaine, both for men, money, and all warlike provision, & either to prevent *Hollanders* for their incursions into the *West Indies*, or to set upon them in their own countries upon any advantage . . .

In another early coranto, there is an appeal to readers to believe in the fastidiousness of the news writer who distances himself from the communication style of the almanac writers and even suggests the need for readers to decide for themselves on the reliability of various accounts where they are in contradiction, without overt authorial or editorial intervention. We see here claims to an extremely liberal trust in the good sense of the reader to distinguish truthful information; claims which take their lead from the service provided by the newsletter writers to their social and political superiors in transmitting information to them together with assurances of minimal editorial interference:

> . . . For I translate onely the Newes verbatim out of the Tongues or Languages in which they are written, and having no skill in Prognostication, leave therefore the judgement to the Reader, & that especially when there are tidings which contradict one another. (*Mercurius Britannicus*, No. 28, 28 June 1625)

By 1632 the power of the state was wielded to suppress all corantos and newsbooks. As a consequence, there was then a flood of news ballads since there was an obvious market for news and a pool of printers willing to take the risk of printing it. Gathering momentum was also, in

Siebert's resonant phrase: 'the low rumble of the demand of the people to see, hear and to know . . .' (Siebert, 1965: 87).

Parliamentary reporting: Informing the reader

The great political shift which allowed for an unprecedented experimentation with the form and content of news production in print came as a consequence of the summoning of the Long Parliament on 3 November 1640. At first, members of Parliament sought to have their speeches, or their opinions, published and circulated by sympathetic printers but textually they retained the general attributes of elite communication (Mendle, 2001: 59). However, as the crisis deepened into rebellion and due to the civil war from the early 1640s onwards, there was a radical reorientation of interest in current affairs and the discussion of ideas in the midst of which the publication of contemporary debate on politics in newsbooks came to represent the interests of popular politics against authoritarianism (Raymond, 1996: 82). The confusion of conflicting accounts drew in readers wanting to get closer to an accurate assessment of the positions and claims of both sides. In this volatile climate, the production of domestic news multiplied. From the 1640s, newsbooks claimed exact dates for their news and contained domestic news and unchanging titles, which gave them a greater sense of continuity. The distribution networks which had been built by the corantos and newsletters meant that there was a ready market and supply infrastructure for the innovation of the newsbook. The first publication of the proceedings of both Houses of Parliament was the *Heads of Severall Proceedings in this Present Parliament from the 22 November to the 29* in 1641. This was the first recorded English newsbook. It consisted of eight pages and included both domestic and foreign news although, in keeping with the times, it was predominantly a retelling of events and discussions in Parliament. It was ordered into chronological headings and was the composite work of a writer, an editor and a publisher. It attempted to demonstrate a high level of accuracy and impartiality:

> Monday in the House of Commons they received letters from *Ireland*, intimating that theire troubles are so great, that they have scarce time eyther day or night to write. That the Rebells doe much increase and presse hard toward *Dublin*, which putteth the Kingdom into great feare being scarce able to resist them. That they want mony to pay their Souldiers already entertained.
> That sending to the Rebels to demande the cause of theire taking up of Armes, they return a remonstrance that is to maintaine the Kinges prerogative and the freedome of Concience, in the exercising

of religion, which if they may have confermed by Acte of Parliament they will lay down theire Armes, and make restitution for the harmes done by them.

It was with the production of the newsbooks that we begin to see the forensic scrutinizing of the proceedings of Parliament ushering in a 'symbolic leap in attitudes towards the polity' (Raymond, 1996: 122) and the first attempts to consolidate that scrutiny through putting it into a widely accessible and regularly available public form of language as a contribution to a newly 'energized politics' which indicated the extent to which these newsbooks had had broken through the former limits of political experience (Zagorin, 1969: 206). The newsbooks were characterized by being relatively inexpensive, weekly (periodic) and by containing reports of parliamentary proceedings and debate. Initially, they eschewed the pamphlet style of vicious prose or the satirical approach of the ballad. By way of contrast, they attempted to capture the spoken nature of debate in as authentic an account as possible to distinguish their content as news. Public dissemination of regular reports on the contemporary world as well as opinion on those events and the political personalities involved, constituted in itself a radical break with traditions of language use and it was to provide the beginnings of a reconfigured relationship between public communication and social and political worlds. The distinguishing features of this language, conceptually speaking, were a concentration on the contemporary and the strong sense of a social audience. This latter point was profoundly political as it challenged previously established hierarchies of communication even if the information was not strictly speaking about politics or if it tried to be as even-handed as possible when dealing with political issues.

As political tensions increased, so too did the numbers of newsbooks and consequently plagiarism between competing titles as all attempted to provide the latest and most complete news for their readers. The *Perfect Diurnall* was launched on 3 July 1643 with a strategy of rational, evidence-based appeal to its readers as equals:

> . . . You may henceforth expect from this relator to be informed onely of such things as are of credit, and of some part of the proceedings of one or both houses of Parliament fit to be divulged, or such other news as shall be certified by Letters from the Army, and other parts from persons of speciall trust . . .

The early *Perfect Diurnall* of Samuel Pecke used a form of shorthand, gave examples of extracts, cross-checked its sources and provided calls to the readers as 'people' as participants in the political processes, all in an attempt to create as persuasive a case as possible for its own legitimacy and reliability. It boasted a reputation as a 'competent record of public events' (Frank, 1961: 43) for the very good reason that:

> A reputation for truthfulness and a concern to avoid antagonizing those in power continued to be the route to success among all editors and publishers who did not conspicuously ally themselves with a partisan group; and Pecke, having sampled jail, never again fell off the political tightrope. (Frank, 43)

The newsbooks also developed in terms of their visual presentation. On 3 January 1643 in the *Kingdomes Weekly Intelligencer* there were short phrases indicating the content of reports printed inside. This forerunner of the headline was soon widely copied. More publications sought to trade on claims for the exactitude of their reporting with an increasing number of titles reflecting this in their claims to be a *True Diurnall*, an account of *Diurnall Occurrences* or a *True and Exact Relation*. This was not to last for long. Yet despite these early good intentions, their detractors still found them to be 'false and scandalous' and even these attempts at impartiality were perceived by the existing hierarchy to be an affront to the monarch's presumed monopoly on political leadership.

Ironically, the power and reach of the newsbooks grew still further as their reputation for fairness and balance declined. The audience clearly approved of partisanship which helps to explain the continuities between newsletters and the later newsbooks and mercuries in contributing to the polarization which generated a confrontational view of the world of politics (Cust, 1986: 87). The newsbooks became more opiniated and therefore more individuated, moving rapidly from the sober reporting of 1641 to the battles of the mercuries from 1643. They sought out and talked to the readers in a confident voice with growing consistency of opinion and increasingly addressed them as explicitly colluding in the creation of partisan political positions. Frank has estimated that by the first week of 1644 there were a dozen competing papers providing half the literate males in metropolitan London with a regular supply of news, making them an important force in moulding public opinion (Frank: 57). While most were targeted at metropolitan readers, there were a few short-run papers which sought to exploit the taste for news among specific rural communities. There was an even more obvious political variety of viewpoint with Royalist, Parliamentarian, Presbyterian and Independent papers all identifiable.

The Mercuries: Polemical positions

Mercurius Aulicus (Oxford) was started on 8 January 1643 to counter the London newsbooks and what the Royalists considered parliamentary propaganda despite the newsbooks' early attempts at even-handedness. It was produced first by Heylin and then more emphatically by Sir John Berkenhead with much editorial commentary and counteraccusations of inaccuracies in its rivals' reporting. By 1648, in an edition 'printed in the weeke, in which the Saints looke bleake' (7 August), it included a poetic editorial to fit with the apocalyptic mood:

> . . . Loe now surviving Aulicus appears,
> (Like stormbred Orion, from the angry skie)
> Possessing Traytours with immortall fears,
> Thundered from Joves supremast Majesty:
> Heavens have decreed this, and therefore know,
> You must adjourne from Earth to sit below
> In darkest dungeon of the Stygian pit,
> To vote and order what the Fiends think fit.
> There, Flames shall be your guard, and Hell your Court,
> Where you shall act to make Grand Pluto sport.

And between pages 3 and 7 of this edition from 1648 we can read a fine example of the sort of personal invective hurled at the parliamentary politicians:

> The State Black-smiths, and forgers of the cause have been almost eight years hammering out a pretty Antimonarchical Idoll, and now (like Prometheus) they endeavour to give it life, though it endanger their own . . . O for ever may the name of this Parliament be a bull-beare and hob-gobling to fright and amaze children . . . Fathers of falsehood, Legions of lyes . . . dying their tongues in bloodred blasphemy . . . black Tom, Sir gouty-foot *Thomas*.

One of the most notable of the mercury writers of the period was Marchamont Nedham who demonstrated a remarkable pragmatism in shifting between Parliamentarian and Royalist publications and back while managing to maintain an ability to articulate, through his network of contacts, a style of news cut to suit the tastes and opinions of different political constituencies. He started his career with the co-editorship from 1643 of *Mercurius Britanicus: Communicating the Affaires of Great Britaine: for the Better Information of the People*. His style contributed much to the development of an opinionated, colourful and vitriolic journalism of political engagement including personalized invective, here directed at Birkenhead:

> Thou mathematical liar . . . I tell thee thou art a knowne notorious forger: and though I will not say thou art (in thine own language, the sonne of an Egyptian whore), yet all the world knows thou art an underling pimpe to the whore of Babylon, and thy conscience an

arrant prostitute for base ends. (*Mercurius Britanicus,* 27 January to
3 February 1645)

Nedham can be seen in the following, playfully exploiting the range of
opinion on the whereabouts of the King, as if weighing them up from
the perspective of the conscientious editor while deploying the various
explanations as a satirical device before going on to indulge in what
would become a staple of more modern popular journalism, the offer of
a reward for information provided:

> Where is King *Charles*? What is become of him? The strange
> variety of opinions leaves nothing certain: for some say, when he
> saw the Storm coming after him as far as *Bridgwater,* he ran away
> to his *dearly beloved* in *Ireland*; yes, they say he *ran away* out of
> his own *Kingdome* very *Majestically*: Others will have him erect-
> ing a new *monarchy* in the Isle of *Anglesey*: A third sort there
> are which say he hath hid himselfe. I will not now determine the
> matter, because there is such a deal of uncertainty; and therefore
> (for the satisfaction of my Countrymen) it were best to send *Hue
> and Cry* after him.
>
> If any man can bring any tale or tiding of a willfull King, which
> hath gone astray these foure yeares from his Parliament, with a
> guilty conscience, bloody Hands, a Heart full of broken Vowes and
> Protestations . . . give notice to Britanicus, and you shall be well
> paid for your paines. So God save the Parliament. (*Mercurius
> Britanicus,* No. 92, 28 July to 4 August 1645)

By 1650, Nedham had started to edit the licensed *Mercurius Politicus*
and continued as an important contributor to the development of political journalism in his pioneering of the editorial opinion piece and his
facility for publicizing republican ideas in a language and rhetoric
which combined political sophistication with an ear for a vernacular
appeal to a broad readership. This was often couched in remarkably
prescient historical contextualizations of topical issues which aimed at
establishing the national interest in republican terms:

> The Majesty of *England,* (though now diffused in the hands of
> many) is the same as it was, when in the hands of one; and is indeed
> much more majestick now, than it hath been for many hundred
> years past . . . free from the check of any *single Tyrant* . . .
>
> Above all, it concerns such a Commonwealth as ours to beware of
> any the most petit insinuations (either at home or abroad) that may
> open the least Cranie to let in so much as a *little finger* of a *banisht
> Tyrant,* or *Tyrannick Family*; for, admit that, and then the whole
> Body follows, and what not? *Revenge* is reckoned *inter Arcana
> Imperii,* one of the speciall mysteries in the Cabinet-Counsels of

Royalty, and prized as the prime Jewell of a *Crown* . . . (*Mercurius Politicus*, No. 39, 27 February to 6 March 1651)

In effect, the period 1640–1660 is an extended experiment in the politics of the press under conditions which swing from almost absolute freedom to almost absolute control. Despite this, however, as with Milton in his famous *Areopagitica* (1644) most polemicists really only wanted freedom for those whose opinions concurred with their own. For the philosophical stirrings of a genuine freedom of the press we must turn to the Levellers. In 1648, *The Moderate* was launched as a forum for Leveller discussion and debate. Its author, Mabbott, used a language of straightforward appeal to engage readers in radical ideas about democratic participation and provide an alternative narrative on the chaos of contemporary military and political events which provides a striking illustration that the development of the language of the news was a struggle between oppositional forces. Frank argues that it used the slogan '"Salus populi suprema lex" as a leftist battle-cry . . .' (Frank, 1961: 156) with their petition to parliament of 11 September 1648 as possibly the high point of its public polemic.

Another significant periodical with an ability to fashion compelling explanations from the perspective of a popular position was Dillingham's *Moderate Intelligencer* again stressing the importance of 'plain English' to political debate:

> Governments (to lay aside the terms of Monarchy, Aristocracie, and Democracie, as words too hard for most) are either when the people . . . choose or appoint one supream magistrate wrest not the Law to their hurt, nor that any foreign power invade, oppresse, or subject them, and then he is qualified with power (yet bounded) and with revenue because chief, & in this way the highest is no more of God then the lowest (for what ever God enjoyns as morall, is binding to all reasonable creatures) nor freer from questioning, some say: This way of a King, which English word, as they that understand the Saxon language say, signifies no more but cunning: A cunning or wise man is set over the people by their consent, because cunning, to see to their preservation.
>
> The second is when the King is set aside, and the government by Lords and Commons, to speake plain English, hath the same trust the King had, which hath beene, as to action divers years past, and this seems to claim its place if an alteration.
>
> The third is to have the government of Commons onely, which, *de facto*, it's now coming unto, as appears by the ensuing Votes, which past in the House of Commons. (*Moderate Intelligencer*, No. 199, 4 January to 11 January 1649)

Generic variations

Given that the events of the Civil War so subverted ordinary people's beliefs and expectations of the natural and God-given political order, it is not surprising that they flocked to read accounts of a world turned upside down to help them find at least confirmation in these accounts that the world had gone mad. Life was beyond the rational control of men. Omens, monsters, portents, prognostications, storms, leap out of the almanac and into contemporary news heralded by such titles as: *Strange and Wonderful Relation, True Relation, Strange News, A Sign from Heaven, Fearful News, News from the Dead.* These stories of the strange and the supernatural often had moral overtones and reinforced notions of social right and wrong for their audiences (Friedman, 1993: 29). In 1647, *The World Turned Upside Down, or, A Brief Description of the Ridiculous Fashions of These Distracted Times* captured the feelings of many in apocalyptic verse commentary:

> Nay, England's face and language is estranged,
> That all is Metamorphis'd chop'd and chang'd.
> For like as on the Poles of the World is whorl'd
> So is this Land the Bedlam of the World. (Friedman: 38)

The newsbooks were responding to changing cultural and political circumstances in the country and in their turn adapting themselves to best exploit the situation and the tastes of their readers. Most news-books came to include some human-interest items, ranging from the weird and the wonderful to the pathos of a country torn apart by civil war. In the newsbooks there was an experimentation with form and genre. John Crouch provided a ribald variant on the news of the day in his *Man in the Moon* from 1649 and his *Mercurius Fumiogus* (1654). The generic variety of many of the newsbooks allowed satirical content the foreground while the content could range from reporting in straight prose, to dialogue and ballad poems.

Pamphlet plays, according to Wiseman (1999) present themselves to their readers as both news and politics, indicating an early problem in distinguishing news from opinion and illustrating the variety and blending of hybrid styles in the production of the print culture of England from a very early stage. He claims they provided, '. . . a highly hybridized and flexible new type of pamphlet, sitting at the borders of print and oral culture, political theory and polemic, plays and news' (Wiseman, 1999: 69). They were often bound together with newsbooks to further indicate the mingling of genres. They, like more formal news categories, addressed their readers as participants in the vibrant dialogue of political formation as citizens which characterized this

30

period of print culture's emergence. They had a further effect in promoting further debate in printed form because of their controversial and provocative illustration of many of the debates of the day. Dialogue was a staple of both pamphlet and mercury and was intended as a contribution to the news by the editors and writers. One of the best-known writers of these pamphlet plays was Richard Overton. In his *Articles of Treason* (1641): '. . . a dialogue between Master Papist "a profest Catholike" and Master Newes "A Temporiser", the connotations of news as a "temporiser", mediating between publication and public and turning the times to its own advantage, as political opinion and as commodity, is at the core of the way playlets popularized political debate and were also genericized as news in the 1640s' (Wiseman, 1999: 68).

Dialogue was also set down from life by reporters for their readers deploying increasingly systematized methods of note taking to enhance accuracy and thereby claims to authenticity. Trials and executions were noted in an early variety of shorthand, enabling competing accounts to be compiled which were often contrasted by printers and publishers to produce a comprehensive version. Writers of news were quite literally reporting on events and their proximity to the events made their accounts all the more credible with both readers and printers. The reproduction of extempore dialogue (Mendle, 2001: 66) matched the increasing use of the patterns of spoken language in such reports to make them sound more lifelike as promised in the title of this pamphlet:

> The Arraignment and Acquittal of Sr. Edward Moseley Baronet, Indicted at the Kings bench for a Rape, upon the body of Mistris Anne Swinnerton. January 28, 1647. Taken by a Reporter there present, who heard all the Circumstances thereof, whereof this is a true Copy. (London 1647)

Another form of generic variation within news dissemination was the almanac. Almanacs were also an increasingly popular form of intervention in the political debates of the time. In a world in which normal expectations were being blown away with alarming regularity, people turned to the almanac and its apocalyptic language as a means of discovering the truth within events. Censorship had reduced the political content of the almanac through Elizabeth's reign but during the Civil War it leapt back to prominence as it provided another indicator of the need of people for some form of explanation and reassurance about the patterns of the future and the relationship of the present to that future which the almanac claimed to provide. William Lilly, politicizing astrology, provided predictions from a parliamentary perspective in *The Starry Messenger, or, An Interpretation of Strange Apparitions*

(1644). In keeping with the wide variety of periodical publication, almanacs were aimed at a general audience and 'drew ideas and assumptions from higher intellectual levels, and presented them in a cheap and digestible form to a far wider readership' (Capp, 1979: 283).

Conclusion

By the time of the Commonwealth 1649–1651, it has been observed that 'Journalism, controlled or uncontrolled, had become a permanent social and political phenomenon' (Siebert, 1965: 220). Both the newsbooks and the mercuries provide us with an initial perspective on how public communication could be used to both report and simultaneously influence social and political changes. We have, even at this early stage in the evolution of the newspaper, a twin-track of experiments with direction. The language of the more measured journalism of the period, in fact, contributes to the rational, Enlightenment idea of knowing the causes of things and having rational opinions on current affairs. The language of most of the mercuries and popular prints such as the almanac and pamphlet plays of the time illustrate how the supernatural and the irrational were expressed as a common, popular and everyday discourse. The development of bourgeois periodical publications was eventually to erode the irrationality of some of the output of the Civil War period's mercuries and broadsides but leave sedimentations of these trends in the sensationalist and melodramatic traditions of later popular publications.

2 Putting on a style: The contours of a public sphere

Introduction

The language of the periodical press after 1660 developed as a pragmatic negotiation between the demands of first, readers, who increasingly perceived themselves as both private individuals and as part of a wider public; second, printers and advertisers, who were also keen to profit from wider circulation; third, politicians, who had an ambivalent attitude to exposure in the news, fearful of criticism yet dependent upon the popular legitimation which the newspapers could provide them with.

The point to stress early on in this chapter is that the newspaper developed unevenly after the Restoration as, in effect, a series of experiments in probing the boundaries of bourgeois good taste in cultural matters, at the same time as it was testing the tolerance of the political elite with regard to criticism and commentary on policy. The wide range of generic variety within these experiments confirms that the newspaper continued with a diversity of content and appeal in order to retain its readers. For their part, the elite classes could, in theory, control newspapers and they were able to demonstrate this at times over the next 200 years through subsidy, taxation, suppression and prosecution but they were also keen to be associated with the rhetoric of freedom which the newspapers increasingly claimed as their own. They were confident that they could manipulate sections of this new communicative form ('newspaper' as a term is first recorded in 1670) to present their own perspectives in as persuasive a manner as possible and thereby garner popular support while being able to take action against seditious influences when they saw fit.

Post-restoration newspapers

After the 1662 Printing Act, Lestrange became the Surveyor of the Press and was granted a monopoly on official news. There was only one official government newspaper. The *Oxford Gazette* containing official announcements but also overseas news was published twice weekly between 1665 and 1666 until it moved back to plague-free London and became the *London Gazette*. In Lestrange's hands, the report became the dominant form of newspaper content once again. In its claims to authority and its structured formality, the *Gazette* is very distant in style and political ambition from the vitriol of the mercuries of the Civil War years. It is also a precursor of the professionally distanced style of news writing which would remain the staple of mainstream newspaper style until the late nineteenth century in England. It was produced in an entirely different format from the earlier newsbooks. It was a half sheet with two columns on each side, thus making more economical use of paper. It provided a combination of court and foreign news and had a good reputation for these, especially its foreign service, because of its privileged access to diplomatic sources. Herd has claimed that

> In the history of journalism its significance lies in the fact that its single leaf form (technically a half sheet in folio), with its pages divided into two columns, broke away from the news-pamphlet form to a style that is a recognizable link with the newspaper as we know it today. (Herd, 1952: 33)

Despite limitation to one official publication, the fact that the government felt obliged to produce its own official newspaper at all is a mark of how news-oriented English society had become in the preceding twenty years (Woolf, 2001: 98). Lestrange himself articulated this social solution to a political problem:

> Tis the *Press* that has made 'um *Mad*, and the *Press* must set 'um *Right* again. The Distemper is *Epidemical*; and there's no way in the world, but by *Printing*, to convey the *Remedy* to the *Disease*. (*Observator*, No. 1, 13 April 1681, quoted in Raymond, 1999: 109)

The *London Gazette* was however handicapped in the public eye because of its lack of the domestic political news which continued to be officially outlawed. To fill this gap, a rival of Lestrange's, Muddiman, continued with an influential weekly newsletter which drew upon an impressive range of social and political contacts who could provide a wider and less proscribed range of information than the official newspaper. As a consequence, this kept pressure on the official publication to maintain a freshness of appeal to its subscribers. There had been such newsletters from the 1630s in England, particularly following the introduction of a weekly post in 1637 but the difference, as Sutherland claims, is that 'Muddiman brought it to a point of efficiency, both in its contents and its circulation, that it had never reached before' (Sutherland, 1986: 6).

Profits, partisanship and the public

Between 1678–1682, fears that there were plans afoot to manipulate a Catholic succession to the throne, known as the 'Popish Plot', led to bitter political in-fighting which produced the parliamentary division between Whigs and Tories. There was a marked increase in the production of newspapers and newsletters after the lapse of press controls in 1679 with 17 titles coming out between that point and 1682, most notably those with the word 'Protestant' in the title, indicating a newspaper of Whig orientation. As during the Civil War, partisan publications flourished as there were profits to be made out of political and religious rivalries. These papers demonstrated that there was a suppressed popular demand for political debate in print to which the official newspapers had contributed very little. The following two extracts, on the same front page of the same edition, show how representation of popular political opinion could be reported in the form of a petition while the newspaper also contrived to produce a tragic and poignant tale of domestic violence to maintain a broader news agenda:

> The Protestant (Domestick) Intelligence or, News both from CITY and COUNTRY Published to prevent false reports. Fryday, January 14. 1680.
>
> January, 13. 1680. A Common Council was held at *Guild Hall*, to whom this day several Eminent citizens presented a petition, which is (*verbatim*) as followeth.
>
> The humble Petition of the Citizens and Inhabitants of the said City.
>
> Sheweth,
>
> That we being deeply sensitive of the evils and mischiefs hanging over this Nation in general, and this City in particular in respect of the danger of the Kings person, the Protestant Religion, and our well establish'd Governemnt by the continued hellish and damnable designes of the papists and others and their adherents: And knowing no way (under heaven) so effectual to preserve his Royal Majesty (and 'tis) from the utter ruin and destruction threatened; as by the speedy sitting of this present Parliament, the surprising Prorogation of which greatly adds to and increases the just fears and jealousies of your Petitioners minds . . .
>
> From *Kent-Street*, in the Parish of St. *Georges-Southwark*, we have this following Relation, That on Tuesday last, a Servant-maid was so prevailed with by the Seducements of the Devil, as to attempt the Murther of her Masters Child which she had in charge; whereupon she carrying it up stairs, got a knife, and putting the same to the Throat of it, began to eat it; but whether by the Remorse of Conscience, or by reason of the crying of the Child she feared some body would surprise her in the fact; she let the knife drop out of her

hand after she had cut about a quarter of an inch deep, and then seeing the Infant bleeding, she took a Dose of Poison, (as she has since reported) prepared to end her wretched Life . . .

Heraclitus Ridens; Or, a Discourse between Jest and Earnest, where many a True Word is spoken in opposition to all Libellers against the government first appeared on 1 February 1681, and continued once a week to 22 August 1682. It demonstrated that commentary on contemporary political issues, couched in an accessible dialogue format reminiscent of the playlets of the Civil War was a viable commercial proposition for the printer and clearly found a ready readership. Sutherland has commented that it was 'written in colloquial English, but addressed to readers of some politeness who could appreciate a witty turn of phrase' (Sutherland, 1986: 18).

Between 1694 and 1695, the printing Act lapsed once more and for the final time. Any form of pre-publication regulation had become impossible to police by this point because of King William's difficulties in maintaining control of printing in a bipartisan parliament and on account of the fact that printers were increasingly willing to challenge the monopoly of the Stationers' Company by pandering to profitable public taste. In 1695 *The Post Boy, The Flying Post, The Post Man* were quick to capitalize on this. They were published three times a week on Tuesday, Thursday and Saturday, to match the days when the mail left London in the evenings to maximize distribution to the rest of the country. Restrictions in the supply of news often meant, however, that early issues were limited to a single page. In order to supplement a variable flow of what we might call nowadays 'hard' news, miscellany was once more a prominent feature into the early eighteenth century as reports from home and overseas, contributions from readers in the form of letters, religious news, cultural commentary, shipping and commercial news all vied for the attention of an inquisitive public. There were experiments in form as well as frequency with one of the most notable being, Ichabod Dawks experiment from 1696 in his *Dawks's News-Letter*. This was an evening newspaper which was notable for its use of a script which mimicked a handwritten style, designed to bring, he hoped, something of the personal tone of the handwritten newsletter to his new printed newspaper.

The *Daily Courant* of 1702 is recorded as the first regular English daily newspaper and it is the regularity of its appearance which makes it a significant element in the development of journalism. It was a half sheet on one side of paper, with two columns all made up of foreign, second-hand news. It developed over the first months of its production into 4 to 6 pages and came to include advertising and shipping news. Its advantage lay in the access to reliable foreign intelligence which was guaranteed by its editor's (Samuel Buckley) access to extensive news sources of the Secretary of State's office (Harris, 1987: 156). This dependence on the proximity of any reliable daily newspaper to government sources and dependence on the good opinion of those same sources for its continuing privileges was to remain a handicap to the newspaper's wider social and political independence for many years.

The eighteenth century has been described as one of 'increased social intercourse' (Siebert, 1965: 305) and the newspaper played an important part in this process of socialization. This was particularly pronounced in their contribution to a language of debate which can be said to have moulded 'public opinion' (Barker, 1998). Yet it was the review format, developing in parallel with the newspaper, which enabled authors to begin to educate readers into political and cultural debates. Central to the review form were authors such as Defoe, Addison and Steele who in their contrasting ways fashioned a public ready for a more regular engagement with social debates through the development of a language which sought to encourage the participation of its targeted readers in these debates within a rhetoric of inclusivity.

Daniel Defoe: The *Review*

Daniel Defoe was a writer whose abilities spanned fiction as well as periodical publication and his journalism would be classified today as opinion or editorial rather than news, but at this juncture the distinction between these genres was uncertain (Milic, 1977: 36). Nevertheless, he insisted that his style should be as clear as possible to better effect that persuasion:

> If any man was to ask me what I would suppose to be a perfect style or language, I would answer, that in which a man speaking to five hundred people, of all common and various capacities, idiots or lunatics excepted, should be understood by them all. (Herd, 1952: 51)

He was regarded as a skilful enough communicator by first minister Harley to be sponsored for his periodical writing in order to propagate government views. The resulting *Review* from 1704 provided foreign news as part of political commentary and indeed political preferences on issues of economic policy and trade formed the backbone of the publication. The original full title of his review indicates the level of rivalry between competing accounts of the contemporary world which jostled for public attention in this period as well as the appreciation of the need to provide something lighter as an addition to the mixture:

> A REVIEW of the Affairs of FRANCE and all of EUROPE . . . Purg'd from the Errors and Partiality of *News-Writers* and *Petty-Statesmen*, of all Sides. WITH AN Entertaining Part in Every Sheet, BEING, ADVICE from the Scandal. CLUB, To the Curious Enquirers; in Answer to Letters sent them for that Purpose.

He, characteristically, addresses the stylistic exigencies of treating matters of economic and political importance, highlighting the need for a mode of address which suits his subject matter and claiming expertise and authority in these areas while appreciating that there are other more scientific matters which he will be pleased to take advice on with regard to the appropriateness of language:

> Let not those gentlemen who are critics in style, in method or manner, be angry that I have never pulled off my cap to them in humble excuse for my loose way of treating the world as to language, expressions, and politeness of phrase. Matters of this nature differ from most things a man can write. When I am busied writing essays and matters of science, I shall address them for their aid and take as much care to avoid their displeasure as becomes me; but when I am on the subjects of trade, and the variety of casual story, I think myself a little loose of the bonds of cadence and perfections of style, and satisfy myself in my study to be explicit, easy, free, and very plain. (*Review*, Vol. 1, Preface, February 1705)

His robust and earthy prose style is ideally suited to the communication of the salient points of commerce in the burgeoning colonial economy of early-eighteenth-century England and his celebration of the power of capital to create the structures of bourgeois civic identity reads like a popularization of the civil society of the human subject through rights in property espoused by philosophers such as Locke:

> Mr Review Plumps For Free Trade
>   . . . I wonder sometimes at the ignorance of those people and nations whose gentry pretend to despise families raised by trade. Why should that which is the wealth of the world, the prosperity and health of kingdoms and towns, be accounted dishonourable? If we respect trade, as it is understood by merchandising, it is certainly the most noble, most instructive, and improving of any way of life . . . the merchant makes a wet bog become a populous state; enriches beggars, ennobles mechanics, raises not families only, but towns, cities, provinces, and kingdoms. (*Review,* Vol. 3, No. 2, 3 January 1706)

Addison and Steele: The *Tatler* and the *Spectator*

Despite the range and impact of Defoe's commentary on politics and commerce, the experimentation with form and style in the periodical press was most fully cultivated in the early century in the work on the *Tatler* and the *Spectator* by Steele and Addison which most succinctly represented the cultural concerns of the rising bourgeois class and provided it with a guide to taste and manners. The *Tatler* began in 1709, appearing three times a week as a folio half sheet and costing a penny. Its initial author, Steele, had been a successful playwright and he contributed a good ear for the patterns of polite conversation and argument into the pages of his publication leading commentators to observe: '. . . its tone was simple – conversational' (Graham, 1926: 65). From the start, it was clear that chasing after the latest news was not going to be its forte: '. . . we shall not, upon a dearth of news, present you with musty foreign edicts, or dull proclamations . . .' (*Tatler*, No. 1, 12 April 1709).

From the seventh edition, he began soliciting letters to the editor, news was dropped from number 83 in the face of fierce competition from specialist newspapers and the readership was cultivated in a complex construction of taste, opinion and manners. Strong editorial coherence contributed to its success and was provided with the fictional character of Isaac Bickerstaff as the porte parole of the authors. All the features of the *Tatler* had been seen before but it was in the overall tone and ambition of the journal to mould polite taste that made it distinctive. It has been observed that:

> The *Tatler* has more of the tone of the coffee-house, even of the tavern. It appealed, and was designed to appeal, more to the fashionable world. (Ross, 37)

To this end, it presented a calm and gentle style of debate far removed from the invective of party politics or the opinionated certainties of the old aristocratic classes and sometimes alluded to this in subtle fashion in its commentary as when Steele writes on duelling:

> A letter from a young lady, written in the most passionate Terms, wherein she laments the Misfortune of a Gentleman, her Lover, who was lately wounded in a Duel, has turned my Thoughts to that Subject, and enclined me to examine into the Causes which precipitate Men into so fatal a Folly . . . it is worth our Consideration to examine into this Chimaerical groundless Humour, and to lay every other Thought aside, till we have strip'd it of all its false Pretences to Credit and Reputation amongst Men. (*Tatler*, 4 June to 7 June 1709)

The *Spectator* appeared daily from March 1711 to December 1712 and continued to eschew news as a staple. Editorial coherence was provided through the character of the enigmatic figure of the 'author' Mr. Spectator and it was addressed to the morning tea-table, to the reflective hours of the civil servants and merchants represented in its subscription list (Ross, 1982: 37). The characterizations, personalization of issues of taste, good manners and good opinion, which were developed in these two periodicals, contributed to a general cultural appreciation of the motivations of individuals and of social self-interest. These in turn, it has been argued, contribute to the psychological mechanisms of the early novel (Watt, 1957; Hunter, 1990; Black, 2008) and in their periodic style also to the initial picaresque of early narrative conventions within the novel. Davis (1983) argues that beyond the periodical, newspapers share with the novel many of the same discursive features of the late seventeenth century drawing as they do upon a related set of narrative and psychological principles.

The polite range of discussion of these periodicals may have been very different in style from the mercuries and the Whig/Tory polemic of the Popish Plot period, yet it still carried a subtle yet potent political ambition within its language and one which was to have long lasting consequences:

> . . . its major impulse is one of class consolidation, a codifying of the norms and regulating of the practices whereby the English bourgeoisie may negotiate an historic alliance with its social superiors. (Eagleton, 1991: 10)

As a complement to their cultural ambitions to foster civilized cultural debate on the contemporary world, the *Tatler* and *Spectator* directed themselves beyond the traditionally narrow appeal to men who were interested in hard political discussion to base their appeal to a female audience, at least in part, and provided a resilient commercial model for this aspect of later popular newspaper miscellanies (Harris, 1987: 179).

Control and resistance

Despite the fact that it was the occasional pamphlets, with their largely uncontrolled and disruptive effects on public opinion, which were the chief target of the Stamp and Advertising Duty legislation which was introduced in 1712, the timing of the legislation indicates that it was finally Samuel Buckley's critical comments in his *Daily Courant* on the conduct of the war with the Dutch which may have ultimately tipped Parliament into action. There was also a strong economic motivation. In addition to concerns over the influence of erroneous or seditious material, at the start of the eighteenth century, there was a pressing need for the government to raise funds via commodity taxation and newspapers by this time very conveniently fell into this category. Such taxation was to play a formative role in the shaping of newspaper language until its eventual lifting in the mid-nineteenth century.

There were many experiments in the format of the emerging newspaper of the early eighteenth century which sought to probe the political potential of the medium. In an early example, the *London Journal* called for an investigation of the South Sea Bubble investment disaster and 'public justice' for the managers of the scheme. Its most venomous pieces were signed CATO. By 12 August 1721, it was selling 10,000 copies per edition. Cato combined calls for compensation with warnings against what he perceived as attempts to reintroduce restrictions on press freedoms, moving as in the example below from the general to the particular in terms of the machinations of political ministries against the press. His targeting of Walpole's administration was clear and damaging enough in its barb to demand censorious action from the government:

> Without Freedom of Thought, there can be no such Thing as Wisdom; and no such Thing as Publick Liberty . . . Guilt only dreads Liberty of Speech, which drags it out of its lurking Holes, and exposes its Deformity and Horrour to Daylight . . . Freedom of Speech is the great Bulwark of Liberty; they prosper and die together: and it is the Terror of *Traytors* and *Oppressors*, and a Barrier against them . . . All Ministries, therefore, who were *Oppressors*, or intending to be *Oppressors*, have been loud in their complaints against Freedom of Speech and the License of the Press.
> (*London Journal*, 4 February 1720)

Walpole moved swiftly and bought the paper in 1722, dismissed the editors and changed the line of the paper to something more acceptable to the government. Despite this example of political intervention by a regular newspaper, it was the pamphlet form which continued to flourish. Furthermore, it was the unofficial and therefore illegal, irregular and incendiary, hawked material which most benefited from the creation of the category of officially stamped newspapers from 1712. It could undercut officially sanctioned newssheets and had an aura of greater freedom of expression. Periodical news could not have emerged as it did through the middle years of the century if the mainstream press had not felt obliged to enter into competition with this style of unofficial publication in its claims to represent the interests of the public and to provide them with fresh and provocative intelligence and the stirrings of controversy in political debate. Thus the discourse of newspaper language was shaped both inside the mainstream and as a competitive response to forces outside of that mainstream. In a political climate, where, after the 'Glorious Revolution' of 1688, the King was no more than a privileged member of the political establishment, stripped of quasi-divine hereditary rights, the newspapers needed to place the highest priority on persuasion. There was little genuine desire or political motivation to produce impartial accounts particularly of politics:

> The preoccupation of the journalist lay quite outside the accurate reporting of facts; there were no facts more important, nor more urgent, than the fate of factions; it was these that provided the revenue, the market and the intellectual compulsion behind the product. (Smith, 1978: 157–158)

This need for political persuasion is what prompted first Harley and then Walpole (1715–1742) to develop a network of writers and publishers who could be relied upon to accept financial subsidy in return for a wide range of privileged access to information. This made for newspapers which were more useful to political elites than to the generally interested public and meant that disaffection with government came to be articulated through a variety of textual experiments within periodical publications as they sought to test the boundaries of official tolerance.

The *Craftsman*

Critical debate began to work itself into the periodical press once again within the restrictions imposed by the political and editorial control of Walpole. The *Craftsman* was the most famous political essay paper of the period. It emanated from a ruling class which felt its position in the constitution to be threatened by Walpole's apparent monopoly on power and opinion. From 7 December 1726, under the pseudonym of Caleb Danvers, Nicholas Amhurst, a former Whig, was employed by William Pulteney to write in opposition to Walpole and particularly his control of the press. Yet the most significant contributor was a dissenting Tory Lord Bolinbroke. The way that such newspapers operated in providing a textual community of argument targeted against the government has been highlighted in the following terms:

> Like other political newspapers, the *Craftsman* offered its sponsors a variety of benefits, among which the creation of an illusion of group solidarity was one of the most useful. The presentation of argument and comment through the single fictional author helped, however superficially, to conceal the fissures within the heterogeneous opposition. (Harris, 1987: 114)

Its pinnacle of notoriety and provocation came in the form of a letter, reputedly translated out of the Persian language. This was a common strategy in the early eighteenth century for addressing domestic issues while avoiding the official wrath of politicians which would have befallen a more literal approach. On this occasion, the savagery of the satire was enough to cause outrage even in this disguised form as it clearly attacked Walpole and impugned his ambition and reputation for financial probity. It is interesting to read how it sets up the satirical attack by disingenuously claiming that as the author wants to provide more than just dull discourse on political matters, he will provide a translation of an exotic tale from a friend who has recently returned to England after travelling abroad. It was a standard rhetorical device to veil the explicit meaning but one whose opacity still allowed readers to deduce the true target of the satire:

> Having as yet given the Reader little besides grave discourse on publick matters, and foreseeing that, during the Session of Parliament, I shall be obliged to continue daily in the same track, I am willing to take this one opportunity of presenting him with something which has no relation at all to Publick affairs, but is of a nature purely amusing, and entirely devoid of Reflection upon any person whatsoever.
>
> My Friend *Alvarez* (a man not unknown to many here, by his frequent journeys to *England*) did some time since make me a present of a *Persian* manuscript, which he met with while he follow'd the fortunes of *Miriweis*. An exact translation of the first chapter has been made at my request by the learned Mr *Solomon Negri*, and is as follows;
>
> The first Vision of Camilick
>
> In the Name of God, ever merciful, and of *Haly* his prophet. I slept in the plains of *Bagdad*, and I dreamed a dream . . .
>
> In the midst of these execrations enter'd a Man, dress'd in a plain habit, with a purse of gold in his hand. He threw himself forward into the room, in a bluff, ruffianly manner. A Smile, or rather a Snear, sat on his Countenance. His face was bronz'd over with a glare of Confidence. An arch malignity leer'd in his eye. Nothing was so extraordinary as the effect of this person's appearance. They no sooner saw him, but they all turn'd their Faces from the Canopy, and fell prostrate before him. He trod over their backs without any Ceremony, and march'd directly up to the Throne. He opened his Purse of Gold, which he took out in Handfulls, and scatter'd amongst the Assembly. While the greater Part were engaged in scrambling for these Pieces, he seiz'd, to my inexpressible Surprize, without the least Fear, upon the sacred Parchment itself. He rumpled it rudely up, and crammed it into his Pocket. Some of the people began to murmur. He threw more Gold, and they were pacified. No sooner was the parchment taken away, but in an instant I saw that august Assembly in Chains; nothing was heard through the whole Divan, but the Noise of Fetters and Clank of Irons. (The *Craftsman*, No XVI, 23–27 January 1727)

The *Craftsman* became a measure against which newspapers' engagement with political discussion and opposition to government could be assessed and continues to hold a high place in historical accounts:

> This much-admired paper created the expectation of an absolutely relentless journalistic opposition to overbearing authority. (Sommerville, 1996: 133)

Nathaniel Mist

A more consistent, and therefore much more dangerous strategy was used by Nathaniel Mist. He used his papers as a platform to create a highly personal dialogue between politics and his own interpretations of them for his readers. *The Weekly Journal; or, Saturday's Post* began on 15 December 1716, became *Mist's Weekly Journal* in 1725 and continued despite a change of name to *Fog's Weekly Journal* until 1737. Along with the *London Journal*, *Mist's Weekly Journal* was the first to fully explore the potential of regular political essays in a newspaper and such interventions were clearly identified by Mist as of intrinsic concern to any participant interested in public debates:

> There is nothing that concerns the attention of a private man as much, as the actions of persons in the administration of public affairs. (*Mist's Weekly Journal*, 3 February 1728)

Mist was constantly in trouble for his publications until in January 1728 he fled to France to avoid further conflict with the authorities. Thereafter, he continued with *Fog's Weekly Journal* which remained the most prominent anti-Whig paper. It frequently addressed public perceptions of politics and the implicit role of periodicals in bringing scrutiny of that process to their readers:

> It was the saying of a very wise man, that the Speculation of Political Affairs, is a much honester Task, than the Practice of them . . . The people can easily see when their Prince is abus'd by selfish Counsellors; and the Reason is plain, for 'tis they who must feel the Effect of such a Conduct: A Knave in Power may find Means of obscuring Things (at least for some Time), from an indulgent Master; but the Multitude is an Argus with a Thousand Eyes, and some of those Eyes are endued with a most penetrating Sight. (*Fog's Weekly Journal*, No. 6, Saturday, 2 November 1728)

There was a section on Foreign Affairs, but essays in the form of contributions were the most prominent features. Home affairs included crime news and deaths, highwaymen, shipping news, accidents and deportations as had become the pattern in most conventional newspapers of the time. The polemic and the controversy which Mist's publications attracted were popular and attracted advertisers eager to have their products associated with such provocative material which was clearly reaching a comparatively widespread readership because of its political notoriety. It was not all one-way-traffic however and the government made various and repeated attempts to close down dissent, through suppression but also by the harnessing of prominent writers to produce a paper to put it in a good light and to provide it with privileged information and a guarantee of material not available to other publications. In 1735, the government organized the talents of many of its subsidized writers in a single paper, and founded the *Daily Gazetteer*.

The *Gentleman's Magazine*

Despite the government's hopes that the public would be content with news provided through its own sponsored sources, there was an increasing pressure to test the boundaries of acceptable access to public discussion of parliamentary debate, independent of government censure or control. Unlike political commentary which, within the limits of libel and sedition, was developing in the essay papers, Parliamentary reporting flouted the law no matter what its content as it had been outlawed since the Restoration. Such reporting broke out not in the essay paper or the newspaper but in another and newer genre, the miscellaneous magazine. It was a very popular feature so that it was in the interests of periodical publications to find ways around official prohibition. Abel Boyer started the first post-revolutionary reports on Parliament in his *Political State of Great Britain* 1703–1729, which was a monthly publication and only published material from sessions of Parliament which were already complete. It was therefore out-of-date and also expensive. The coverage was also pragmatically tinged towards the government so that it could act as a post-facto rationalization of the power politics of the day.

Edward Cave's *Gentleman's Magazine* from January 1731 provided digests of news, literary and political comment, in response to the feeling that the world was becoming too hectic and too crammed full of things to be able to keep up with them in their original form. To this blend, it added the first reports contemporaneous parliamentary proceedings in issue 5 May 1731. From June 1738, it had taken to the ingenious devices of reporting parliament as a Roman Assembly with politicians sporting classical names such as Tullius Cicero and M. Cato and later the Parliament of Lilliput with, for example, the magnificently ironic heading: 'Prime Minister's Speech from the Senate of Magna Lilliputia' and observations such as: 'Mr Gulliver, astonished at the wonderful conformity between the Constitution of England and Lilliput

. . .' (July 1738). It used techniques such as blanking out key letter of names and using anagrammatic names so that it could not be considered a verbatim report of actual parliament with real politicians. Door attendants were bribed to allow access to reporters who would discreetly record the debates for later regurgitation. It was a huge success, and by 1739 had a circulation of 30,000, which allows us, according to Sommerville, to take it as 'an inventory of the mentality produced by a free press' (Sommerville, 1996: 158).

John Wilkes

The career of John Wilkes (1725–1797) indicates the potential for building bridges between an individual's political motivations and the people using a periodical publication which was able to transmit those interests through direct, topical and powerful writing to a wide and regular readership. From 1762, in his essay paper *North Briton*, Wilkes claimed to champion English liberty and the rights of the individual, particularly through a populist campaign which ridiculed George III's Scottish first minister, Lord Bute. To maximize its populist potential, it based itself within and amplified common fears of the perceived threat of Franco-Scottish Jacobites. From the first edition, its intentions were guaranteed to invoke the wrath of the government and were stated in as plain a language as suited its populist desires to stir up unrest:

> The liberty of the press is the birthright of a BRITON, and has by the wisest men in all ages been thought the finest bulwark of the liberties of this country. It has ever been the terror of bad ministers, whose dark and dangerous designs, or whose weakness, inability, or duplicity, have been detected and shewn to the public in too strong colours for them long to bear up against the general odium. No wonder that such various and infinite arts have been employed, at one time entirely to suppress it, at another to take of the force and blunt the edge of this most sacred weapon, left for the defence of truth and liberty. (The *North Briton*, No. 1, Saturday, 5 June 1762)

Part of Wilkes' self-declared motivation was that the *North Briton* had been brought out to counter the *Briton* being published under the Royal coat of arms. By issue number two, he is already criticizing first minister Bute, his place in parliament and doubting his financial abilities to run the Exchequer. For Wilkes, the Scots are characterized as rebellious by nature and led by despot chieftains. This aggressive vindictiveness reached its crescendo in the notorious number 45 of 23 April 1763:

> A despotic minister will always endeavour to dazzle his prince with high-flown ideas of the *prerogative* and *honour* of the *crown*,

which the minister will make a parade of *firmly maintaining.* I wish
as much as any man in the kingdom to see the *honour of the crown*
maintained in a manner truly becoming *Royalty.* I lament to see it
sunk even to prostitution.

This provides a powerful demonstration of how a newspaper could lay
rhetorical claims to speak on behalf of a nation, reinforcing the point
made by Anderson (1986) about the style of expression being of paramount importance in the legitimation of a nation's claims to existence.
This sort of rhetoric was to have an effect in the construction of both
metropolitan and national identities and could be called upon either
conservatively for patriotic purposes or for radical ends in the case of
Wilkes and others who followed him. Furthermore, despite the fact that
the claims made for the value and status of the 'liberty of the press' were
clearly more a rhetorical conceit rather than anything that could be
demonstrated in fact, the political resonance of the phrase meant that it
was capable throughout the eighteenth century and beyond of rallying
people to its cause and the various motivations of newspaper editors.

When Bute was removed from office on the strength of popular
demand, it was the first time that the press had played such a prominently proactive role in removing a politician from power and showed
that it was possible for opinion to drive the events which become the
news. In addition, despite Wilkes' subsequent exile, the notoriety of the
case meant that in 1765 general warrants, which had long been the bane
of publishers' and political writers' lives and which enabled the authorities to make general sweeps for unspecified material, were declared
illegal, indicating how popular support for Wilkes had made it untena-
ble for the Courts to continue to pursue such prosecutions where they
were unpopular and difficult to pursue to a satisfactory conclusion.

The right to report Parliament was challenged by *The Parliamentary
Spy* in 1769, and *The Whisperer*, in 1770, reported Parliament regularly
and scurrilously. From 1771, once Wilkes' *Middlesex Journal* had faced
down another legal challenge, Parliament could eventually be reported
with impunity. This, combined with other major events of the last quarter of the century such as the American Revolution and the French
Revolution, heightened the political content of the mainstream London
newspapers and their growing credibility to their advertisers as genuinely independent and authoritative organs. There was an increasing
resonance around the discourse of public opinion which the newspapers fed into, often out of the sheer self-interest in presenting themselves
as first and foremost the champions of the public, their customers:

> . . . it is clear that public opinion was increasingly associated with
> those who read newspapers and other forms of printed matter, and

that this was a trend encouraged by the newspapers themselves. (Barker, 2000: 28)

The *Public Advertiser*

One of the most prominent advertising-led periodicals of the period, the *Public Advertiser*, drew most publicity to itself by the publication of readers' letters on matters of political controversy. In addition to its letters, it fitted well within the miscellany of the eighteenth century newspaper which encompassed the results of prize draws, news from various government departments such as Navy Office and Stamp Office, shipping news and gossip from polite society. There was a steady supply of criminal news from the courts as well as news from abroad but it is most renowned for its exchanges of letters on the politics of the day. Letters to newspapers were becoming commonplace by the mid-century, always signed with imposing sounding *noms de plume* such as 'Rusticus', 'Cassius', 'Anglo-Saxon', 'A Wilkite' and 'A True Briton' and some, such as 'Junius', made full use of this anonymous tradition of political commentary and even provocation in the *Public Advertiser* from 21 January 1769. In the issue of 19 December 1769 'Junius' wrote to the King:

> Sire – it is the misfortune of your life . . . that you should never have been acquainted with the language of truth, until you heard it in the complaints of your people. It is not, however, too late to correct the error.

The nineteenth-century historian of newspapers Fox-Bourne assessed the contribution of 'Junius' to the development of newspaper journalism in the following terms, considering he had, '. . . raised journalism to a far more important position than it had ever held before . . .' (Fox-Bourne, 1998: 190).

While these letters were vitriolically critical of monarch and government policy, they had the advantage of adding to the commercial success of the newspaper and within the year they had doubled its sales. The notoriety and success of the letters drew influential correspondents to the newspaper and consolidated its position as an important opinion broker as well as continuing to boost its advertising revenue.

Commercial success and social status

Throughout the eighteenth century, advertising continued incrementally to drive the commercial expansion of newspapers and a front page dominated by advertisements, was becoming the fashion since the advertisers accrued greater influence as their financial input increased. This meant that by the final third of the eighteenth century, newspapers had become established commercially and were becoming more confident in espousing a regular public engagement with political issues than they had been while they had been financially insecure. By the 1760s, more papers were adopting four columns per page yet the increase in wordage facilitated by increasing regularity of news did not immediately lead to improvements in the layout of the paper. The advertisements were more effectively and more imaginatively laid out than the news content, in fact, often being illustrated with woodcuts and deployed in imaginative eye-catching typefaces. The shape and structure of news was nevertheless becoming more systematized. It was laid out into regular grids with titled sections for staples such as: LONDON, PORT NEWS, IRELAND, BANKRUPTS. Large bold capitals signalled the initial letters of stories and reports. There were brief reports on the debates and motions of Parliament. Letters from readers were selected to emphasize an identifiable editorial policy. There were articles of intelligence and postscripts from other leading London papers together with prices, stocks, high water marks, the arrivals and departures of ships, gossip, social commentary, theatre announcements and reviews. Reports on the goings-on at court or in broader elite society had become slightly less deferential and came to include the marriages and deaths of the great and good at home and abroad.

Towards the end of the century, newspaper contents reflected social variety as well as variety in content but newspapers were still predominantly aimed at the prosperous middle classes, concentrating on commercial and financial news. With more time to collect and reflect, the weeklies had more general news and a political article or an essay had become an accepted inclusion on their front page. Although there was an accumulation of oppositional voices in the press towards the end of the century, public opinion remained something which could be dominated quite effectively by: 'those few individuals who could manipulate this newly important discursive political construction through print' (McDowell, 1998: 3). The readership of newspapers may have laid rhetorical claims to include the population as a whole but in effect it was restricted to a predominantly metropolitan middle class.

Cheap, unstamped papers aimed at urban lower classes had been suppressed by law in 1743 meaning that the elite political newspaper did not need to compete with them for trade. Subsequently, there was no attempt by the mainstream newspapers to break into a wider market. They kept their diet restricted to political and economic news in the main and let the unofficial and ephemeral media cater for the lower sections of the population. This segmentation of the market was consolidating a reading public along the lines of social stratification. The political coverage and even commentary of the commercially successful newspaper did not imply that there was much up for discussion. Most pieces reflected a certainty that the reader would share the suppositions and intentions of the author (Black, 1991: 246):

> *To the* Author *of The London Evening Post,*
> SIR,
> OUR Merchants, I perceive, complain heavily, that they can find no sort of vent for the goods and manufactures which they send to the island of Minorca; and say, that the island seems to be ours only in name; for that a number of Frenchmen still reside there, who pour into that place French and other foreign commodities, who enjoy every freedom, and run away with all the trade of that island.
> Now, Sir, if that complaint be true, it calls loudly upon the Ministry for immediate redress; for can any thing be worse policy, than to suffer the trade and commerce of France to increase and flourish in that island to the ruin and destruction of our own? Your's etc.
> BREVITAS
>
> *(The London Evening Post*, Saturday,
> 31 December to Tuesday, 3 January 1764)

Newspaper discussions of politics appeared popular simply because it was extended beyond the tradition narrow elite in contact with the actual business of government. Politics, however, remained in flux, although actual criticism until the French Revolution was only of politicians and of a political system which was perceived as being reformable. There was no call for radical change to the social system or the franchise. The only radical critique came from the Jacobites until the time of the French Revolution. As Black had put it, newspapers were: 'Sympathetic to popular distress but opposed to popular action' (Black, 1991: 272).

The increased take-up of advertising in the later years of the century meant that new newspapers were able to offset the expense of circulation taxes and the *Morning Chronicle*, 1770, *Morning Post*, 1772, and *Universal Daily Register (Times)* 1785 were launched.

John Walter on 1 January 1785 in the *Daily Universal Register* well expressed the thriving miscellany of the contemporary daily newspaper:

> . . . the Register of the times, and faithful recorder of every species of intelligence; it ought not to be engrossed by any particular object; but, like a well covered table, it should contain something suited to every palate; observations on the dispositions of our own and foreign courts should be provided for the political reader; debates should be reported for the amusement and information of those

who may be particularly fond of them; and a due attention should be paid to the interests of trade, which are so greatly promoted by advertisements.

Extending editorial credibility

This increase in revenue also provided the newspapers with the opportunity to extend their credibility as independent sources of information and opinion as it released them from their previous reliance on political insiders to provide them with information in exchange for publication privileges. At the end of the century there was a consolidation of the position of the daily newspaper as a rival to the essay paper in terms of its ability to intervene regularly and effectively in the realm of ideas, opinions and public affairs. The importance of the single owner and his relationship with a strong editor became another key component of the editorial character and consistency of these end-of-century newspapers. The *Morning Chronicle* edited by James Perry and the *Morning Post* edited by Daniel Stuart begin to demonstrate what independent newspapers could achieve. The former was the dominant newspaper of its generation after Perry bought it in 1789 employing Sheridan, Ricardo, Coleridge, Charles Lamb, Sir James Mackintosh, Thomas Moore and William Hazlitt and to be hailed, in retrospect as: 'the greatest paper in England' (Herd, 1952: 91). There was, however, still a lack of professional journalists and consequently newspapers of the 1790s still actively encouraged correspondents to send in items including letters on issues of topical political concern (Black, 1991: 283).

Over the course of the late eighteenth century, public reading of newspapers had become commonplace. Taverns, barbers shops and especially the coffee houses which were spreading at the same rapid pace as the newspaper throughout the land (Pincus, 1995), were all part of a complex network of outlets for newspapers and informal discussion groups which gathered to read and to exchange opinion on their reading matter. Inevitably this broadened the social base of readership from those who could afford to buy and read their own copy to those who could borrow a copy or even listen to others reading aloud. Some newspapers were written in an overtly rhetorical style in order to enhance the effect of reading aloud to groups, drawing upon traditions of orality (Ong, 1982) and this matched other fora for the public dissemination of ideas, the pulpit and the public meeting. The newspapers were beginning to play a role in the education of a population into citizenship with all of the implications and demands of this status. This would have a cumulative effect on broad political education: 'Where pamphlets, prints, ballads and verses were occasional, the newspaper offered the possibility of continuous communication and commentary on political events' (Harris, 1996: 4).

Continuities with older forms of printed and manuscript publications persisted. There were regular reports on assizes and executions especially the adventures of highwaymen which competed with the broadside and ballad versions, while shipping news, diplomatic reports, the correspondence of London merchants, accounts from travellers, and items from foreign diplomats found their way into the spaces of the newspaper as they had once found their way into newsletters of old. There were also experiments in juxtaposing reports or using formats to cross-fertilize other issues in the news. The *London Chronicle* of 14 November to 16 November 1765 shows how the juxtaposition of letters could be used to extend political commentary on news from overseas, in this case an exchange between a North American in London and his friend in America on the developing crisis around the question of American independence: 'The Sun of Liberty is indeed fast setting if not down already, in the American colonies . . .'

From 1792, Fox's Libel Law meant that it would be the jury not a judge who would decide whether something was libellous. This was a key moment in the development of the range of newspaper language and the range of material it could cover without fear of prosecution. From 1793, political and popular attention was dominated by the fact that Britain was at war with France. Newspapers extended their coverage of European news and consolidated their growing assertiveness independent of government by improving their sources, stressing the speed and superiority of their news and using devices to emphasize excitement such as headlines and the late insertion of 'breaking' items of news. The editorial or leading article was a device which enhanced this appearance of autonomy. The leading article started to become part of the increasingly distinct editorial positioning of newspapers. (Black, 1991: 281). This editorializing came to 'lead' the identity and opinion of the newspaper and was carefully designed to fit into both the newspaper's sense of its own identity and the identity of its readership imagined as a whole. It was a powerful commercial tool as well as a potent political weapon.

The provincial press

The eighteenth century saw the rise of the provincial newspaper. The first English provincial newspaper is estimated as having been the *Norwich Post-Boy* from 1701 (Read, 1961: 59). By and large, commercial concerns dominated and they did not attempt to influence local opinion. They certainly did not carry original editorial articles and rarely carried detailed news-reporting even of local events. They did carry a lot in the way of advertisements of local produce and businesses. Yet such commercial interests eventually meant that they were inevitably drawn into increasingly political local debate. Clarke (2004) has argued that these two functions were increasingly in symbiosis. Local regional news was chiefly of a police kind, with advertisements as prominent as they were in the metropolitan press. The regional newspapers began by orienting the metropolitan political and commercial emphasis for local readers and later began to differentiate it socially and politically as the interests of London were not always congruent with the interests of the various regional centres. This became increasingly important as the Industrial Revolution gathered momentum.

The importance of the eighteenth century provincial newspapers developed incrementally as each required an individual voice and an identifiable character in order to reflect the specific nature of the communities which they served and from which they drew their profits. Clarke has also claimed that they played an increasing role in opening up a national consciousness by providing readers (and listeners) with a digest of up-to-date news and opinion as well as providing an extended economic service by advertising a range of books, periodicals, medicines and other goods and services to a non-metropolitan audience (Clarke, 2004: 125).

In the last quarter of the century local newspapers began to fill their pages with more in the way of local news. Hitherto, they had merely provided a rehash of the nationals and become local news enabled provincial identities and local political issues to be more firmly established meaning that a language of local identification and a strengthening of regional identities emerged. Provincial newspapers moved further to encompass the political dimension of local communities (Walker, 2006). The first newspaper in the North to develop the techniques of political commentary through the use of editorials and reporting of local meetings according to Read (1961: 69) was the *Sheffield Register*, published by Joseph Gale from 1787 to 1794. It began by including extracts and paraphrases from radical authors such as Paine, Godwin, Horne and Tooke to further establish its credentials and extended from these to original pieces with the same themes.

On 31 March 1792, the first number of the *Manchester Herald* appeared and it was soon advancing the cause of radicalism in its pages for a local readership:

> As France has now been forced into a war by the conduct of Tyrants, who have presumed to interfere in her internal government; and as the contest is for the Rights of man on the one part, and for the Wrongs of Despotism on the other, so this country is particularly

interested in the event. The great Cause of Liberty demands the steady support of the brave, the just, and the philanthropic – for should oppression triumph, the vengeance of power will know no bounds; Racks and Tortures, Bastilles and Inquisitions, will be the punishment of those who have dared to avow themselves the Friend of Liberty. (*Manchester Herald,* 28 April 1792)

Conclusion

The language of the newspaper begins to consolidate its ability to shape and respond to changes in English society and its economic structures and to contribute to the 'complex interplay between press and popular politics (Barker, 2000: 1).

The language of the newspapers of the eighteenth century had become more adept at articulating the political opinions and commercial requirements of a broadened and more self-assured bourgeoisie. There was still no financial incentive or political motivation for the owners of newspapers to attempt to target the lower classes. The inclusion of the reader both implicitly and, in the form of letters, explicitly, ensured that newspapers contributed significantly to the creation of a national community of taste and opinion.

3 Radical rhetoric: Challenging patterns of control

Introduction

A politically radical press emerged and flourished between the closing years of the eighteenth century and the middle years of the nineteenth century. It may have persisted for relatively short periods of time before economics or political repression forced it to find alternative channels for the energies which it harnessed. However, its influence on the language of newspapers has been much more profound and long lasting. It was the radical papers and pamphlets of this period which were to shape a language that appealed beyond the narrow confines of what had been assiduously developed since 1660 as a bourgeois public sphere. The scene is well set by the words of Olivia Smith:

> The press could record public events and it could enliven debate among the politically involved. But as a means of social communication it was, in the eyes of many, a non-starter . . . The social structures were too solid to admit of any new agency. Journalism was kept from communicating between classes, from spreading its truths in such a way as to allow the crowd to set up in judgement against the governing classes . . . (Smith, 1984: 164–165)

This chapter will explore the ways in which radicals, from Paine onwards, developed a language which appealed directly to a wider range of ordinary readers than public writing had ever attempted before on a periodical basis. These writers drew on a variety of linguistic sources including nonconformist religion (Goldsworthy, 2006), vernacular speech patterns and notions of the 'old corruption' (Hollis, 1970) as well as, in some cases, a sophisticated brand of popular political philosophy. After the success of the American and French Revolutions in opening up popular involvement in politics, English radicalism developed its own rhetorical styles and narratives designed to appeal to popular audiences through the nineteenth century. This chapter will consider certain phases of that language from the early radical pamphleteers such as Wooler and Cobbett to the Chartist newspaper editors.

Early-nineteenth-century newspapers: The language of respectability

Successful daily newspapers in the early nineteenth century had perfected a blend of commercial and political information which was couched in a language and approach which would do nothing to disturb their social or commercial respectability. Their independence was too reliant on their attractiveness to advertisers to want to shake the status quo too violently and these newspapers were still overwhelmingly directed towards the interests and politics of a narrow range of the middle classes. The most celebrated example was the *Times* which refused government subsidies and party patronage and enhanced its reputation for political independence by attracting the advertising revenue which could finance industrial investment such as the steam press and a wider network of correspondents. The 'overwhelmingly commercial pressures' (Black, 1991) on such respectable newspapers were a major factor in their relatively peripheral role in political reform in the nineteenth century according to Gilmartin (1996: 85). Yet they did, in a more subtle way, combine to act upon the nature of public language, informed by their development of an individual editorial voice for their papers (Wiener, 1985) enabling a more holistic representation of an identity in print to emerge.

Divisions between epochs in journalism are rarely if ever neat. As one set of developments were moving newspapers towards commercial respectability and therefore a particular sort of political independence, another, long suppressed, radical impulse was about to gain renewed momentum. From the early nineteenth century, readerships were being increasingly identified along class lines because of increasing literacy levels and a more extensive impetus towards popular political involvement. Previously, it had been assumed that all readers were from a relatively homogeneous middle class but this was about to change. As the radical press emerged, seeking to address its readership as a social class for political purposes, it contested the political status quo. The legacy of these publications was the restructuring of the language of political analysis and to prove a major contribution to the formation of a sense of working-class identity.

The fundamental shifts required in approaches to the language of the ordinary people to enable a radical plebeian public language to become established in the press and the political challenge which such language threw down to the conformity of the bourgeois political settlement of the newspapers of the public sphere has been highlighted by Smith:

> The political and social effectiveness of ideas about language derived from the presupposition that language revealed the mind.

> To speak the vulgar language demonstrated that one belonged to the
> vulgar class; that is that one was morally and intellectually unfit to
> participate in the culture ... (Smith, 1984: 2)

Radical periodicals and newspapers were key to the process of challenging these assumptions by creating a politics which was representative of the interests and lives of ordinary working people in a language designed to appeal directly to them both as political listeners and political agents. The importance of these papers lies chiefly in their formation of the social identity of class (Thompson, 1967) and through the production and consumption of these papers, the working people were reciprocally involved in creating this identity for themselves.

Part of the formative process of nineteenth-century newspapers in England which enabled them to articulate the changing discourses of the popular was the way in which they managed to move from the textual reproduction of an individual voice to the textual reproduction of a communal voice. This involved a shift from speaking on behalf of the people to building a communal form of address in dialogue with them. This was an important part of a rhetorical appeal able to combine the tripartite demands of the popular: well liked by the people, representative of the people, produced on behalf of the people (Williams, 1976).

Unstamped weeklies and radical journalism

Between 1793 and 1819, newspapers played an increasingly strident role in opinion formation and in the polarization of popular political debate throughout the years of revolutionary turmoil in France and the subsequent Napoleonic Wars. In Britain, newspapers provided an up-to-date account of the battles and main events of the Revolutionary Wars and were among the leading voices in campaigning for peace from 1807. The French Revolution had brought in 'democratic and demotic' newspapers (Barker, 2000: 176) which in addition to occasional pamphlets played a significant part in creating mass debate. Gilmartin highlights the growing ambitions of radical reformers to develop a political opposition which would drive a wedge between the people and their oppressors in order to focus attention on the common cause of people against the political establishment. This ambition necessitated a language which could play a direct and material part in the production and shaping of political debate:

> During the Napoleonic Wars and the post-war period of economic
> dislocation and popular unrest, as the established parties mapped a
> considerable terrain of consensus, the radical movement developed

> a style of political opposition that aimed to displace the distinction
> between whig and tory with a more ominous one between the
> people and corrupt government, and to make the press a forum for
> mobilizing this distinction on behalf of radical parliamentary
> reform. (Gilmartin, 1996: 1)

There was, however, competition for the attentions of the lower class
readers with publications such as Hannah More's Cheap Repository
Tracts which were explicitly designed to drive politically seditious
publications from the market and to prevent the spread of radical
opinion. They were priced at a penny or a halfpenny and are estimated
to have sold over two million copies between March 1795 and March
1796. They attempted to provide the rudiments of a moral education
in order to secure loyalty to Christian virtues and were anchored in a
sententious style which did not seek to challenge the more traditional
decorum of language and social subservience expected from the lower
classes.

Thomas Paine: Politics in circulation

The initial generator of the fusion of language and popular political
involvement characteristic of the period was Thomas Paine. If
Wilkes can be considered as a particular journalistic voice of the mid-
eighteenth century, using claims to popularity and an aggressive line in
populist rhetoric to secure his political ends, then Paine had more
altruistic democratic goals which were articulated through the style in
which he tried to engage intellectually with the people as a political
constituency rather than through the language of rabble-rousing populism deployed by Wilkes. Thomas Paine produced three political
tracts which were as influential in their content as they were well as in
the language which they developed as a popular forum for political
debate: 1776 *Common Sense*, 1791 *The Rights of Man*, 1795 *The Age of
Reason*. They put politics into circulation among ordinary people
through their combination of topicality and effective calls to political
action in a language which working people could recognize as representative of their own interests. He demonstrated that print was, '. . .
essentially a publicly accessible and accountable medium of communication, not a tool under the monopolistic control of government,
journalists or printers' (Jones, 1996: 12). The revolutionary impact of
his prose broke the existing conventions of the language of popular
appeal demonstrating that it was possible to have, 'an intellectual
vernacular prose . . . neither vulgar nor refined, neither primitive nor
civilized' (Smith, 1984: 35).

Rights of Man is possibly the best illustration of the relevance of his prose to an English audience, triggered as it was as a polemical response to a notorious pamphlet by Burke on the revolution in France. It is journalistic in intent, to the extent that it is based upon contemporary events and furthermore seeks to persuade readers of a particular interpretation of those events:

> When I contemplate the natural dignity of man; when I feel (for Nature has not been kind enough to me to blunt my feelings) for the honor and happiness of its character, I become irritated at the attempt to govern mankind by force and fraud, as if they were all knaves and fools, and can scarcely avoid disgust at those who are thus imposed upon.
>
> We now have to review the governments which arise out of a society, in contradistinction to those which arose out of superstition and conquest.
>
> It has been thought a considerable advance toward establishing the principles of freedom, to say, that government is a compact between those who govern and those who are governed: but this cannot be true, because it is putting the effect before the cause; for as man must have existed before governments existed, there necessarily was a time when governments did not exist, and consequently there could originally exist no governments to form such a compact with.
>
> The fact therefore must be, that the *individuals themselves*, each in his own personal and sovereign right, *entered into a compact with each other* to produce a government: and this is the only mode in which governments have a right to arise, and the only principle on which they have a right to exist. (Van der Weyde, 1925: 73–74)

He enumerates arguments to gather rhetorical momentum, using an ordinary language laced with specifically English historical references. The writing style seeks to demonstrate in logical, sequential patterns the nature of his argument and the fallacy of taking things as they are or of going with emotion rather than the light of reason. He demands that the reader look anew at how we come to understand the world, deploying italics to emphasize key issues in the discussion. He moves from a personal 'I' to a collective 'we', signalling the construction of consensus and varies, in contrast, the forces opposed to rational debate in terms of abstractions such as 'the government' or impersonal constructions such as 'It has been thought'. There is, throughout, a strong reliance within the rhetoric of his exchanges on the assumption of an equal discursive partnership with his readers, a partnership which draws on shared understanding but also on mutual intellectual respect.

He uses the formula of question and answer to construct a debate with the reader as he manoeuvres from a question to an assertion on behalf of the common people:

> What are the present governments of Europe, but a scene of iniquity and oppression? What is that of England? Do not its inhabitants say, It is a market where every man has his price, and where corruption is common traffic, at the expense of a deluded people? No wonder, then, that the French Revolution is traduced. (Van de Weyde, 1925: 154)

Smith (1984) claims that there are significant continuities between the language of the early radical press and the language of the romantics and their political views on popular culture. Writing of the radical reformist pamphleteer, Thomas Spence, she suggests a link which can be traced beyond his work and the language of Cobbett and others into the nineteenth century:

> Spence's attempts to make English a language that was more available to labourers parallels Wordsworth's and Coleridge's efforts to vindicate the language of rustics. The creative and political necessity of discovering a written vernacular language was hardly the concern of only a literary avant-garde but also of social classes that were demanding to be admitted into what had been defined as 'civilization' . . . (Smith, 1984: 249)

John and Leigh Hunt: Philosophical radicalism

The *Examiner* was founded in 1808 with an explicit commitment to radical principles. It was undeniably intellectual in tone and liberal/progressive in its politics. It prided itself upon its wit and elegance in the spirit of the essayists and pamphleteers of the early eighteenth century. To emphasize its lineage it took a quotation from Pope as its masthead slogan: 'Party is the madness of the many for the benefit of the few'. Despite these continuities, it espoused different goals in different political times. Its middle-class credentials were apparent in its commitment to refuse to include advertisements. This was not, as with the working-class radicals, a form of guerrilla opposition to the system of commodity capitalism which so alienated working people but more, as its prospectus states, to prevent it impairing the newspaper's independence and therefore its credibility. It was proud to be able to include influential radical authors of the day in its pages such as Keats, Byron and Hazlitt and its language was consciously structured by literary cadences. The editors skilfully combined letters, detailed observations from commentators around the country and broader political concerns into their reports to leave readers in no doubt of their position:

THE SLAVE TRADE

The Fourth Report of the Directors of the African Institution alludes to a most shameful violation of the Abolition Acts, which was lately detected in the port of London by the exertions of the institution. (*Examiner,* 30 September 1810)

Yet it was most notable for the precise and eloquent discussion of the vocabulary of political opinion, as in the following case, which brought the opprobrium of the establishment down upon them:

CERTAIN TERMS MAGNANIMOUSLY APPLIED TO THE FRENCH RULER

When people talk of BONAPARTE as the 'usurper' and 'upstart' . . . he is no more the usurper of that throne than the Princes of BRUNS-WICK have been the usurpers of the throne of Great Britain and what will be still more shocking perhaps to the delicate ears of the courtiers is, that the House of NAPOLEON has a better original right to the Crown than half the 'legitimate' Houses on the Continent . . . (*Examiner,* No. 141, 30 September 1810)

It was less in the content than in the style of political debate where both the innovation and the limitations of the *Examiner* as a political weapon could be identified. Gilmartin has argued that 'Hunt's willingness to associate peaceful reform with the rhetorical and cognitive style of the middle class became his point of departure from popular radical opposition' (Gilmartin,1996: 223–224).

This sort of approach can be seen in the Preface after its first year of publication:

. . . The abuses of the French revolution threw back many lovers of reform upon prejudices, that were merely good as far as they were opposed to worse: but every prejudice, essentially considered, is bad, is prejudicial . . . We must shake off all our indolence, whether positive or negative, whether of timidity or of negligence, we must shake of all our prejudices, and look about us; and in this effort we must be assisted by philosophy. (*Examiner,* 31 December 1808)

The issue of 22 March 1812, in which appeared an article that cost the brothers two years' imprisonment, consisted of 16 pages included a 5-page report of Parliament, extracts from the *London Gazette*, editorial articles, many news paragraphs, comments on the opera and on pictures exhibited at the London Institution. It was the first article, 'The Prince on St. Patrick's Day,' which was to bring the authorities' wrath down on the paper. It was reported that at the annual St. Patrick's Day, the toast of 'The health of the Prince regent' was 'drunk with partial applause, and *loud and reiterated hisses.*' . . . The article, after contemptuous reference to the 'sickening adulation' of the Prince Regent in the *Morning Post*, went on:

> What person, unacquainted with the true state of the case, would imagine, in reading these astounding eulogies, that this *'Glory of the People'* was the subject of shrugs and reproaches! – that this *'Protector of the Arts'* had named a wretched foreigner his historical painter, in disparagement or in ignorance of the merits of his own country men! . . . that this *'Exciter of desire'* (bravo! Mesieurs of the Post! – this *'Adonis in loveliness'* was a corpulent man of fifty! In short, that this *delightful, blissful, wise, pleasurable, honourable, virtuous, true,* and *immortal* prince, was a violator of his word, a libertine over head and ears in disgrace, a despiser of domestic ties, the companion of gamblers and demireps, a man who had just closed half a century without one single claim on the gratitude of his country, or the respect of posterity!

The *Examiner* constituted a more cerebral form of radical opposition than that of Spence before Cobbett, Wooler and Hetherington later in the century, lacking as it did a robust vernacular engagement with the broader political interests and activities of working people. The language of the live political platform was something which rather connects the rhetoric of Paine to that of Cobbett. The radical movement demanded a democracy of representation as well as a democracy of expression (Calhoun, 1982: 89) and it was to be the unstamped journals and newspapers which provided what Thompson has termed the 'heroic age of popular radicalism' (1967: 660).

William Cobbett: Forging a people's journalism

Cobbett had little of the philosophical sophistication of Paine or classical allusion of the Hunts but he provided a template for radical political journalism which was even more influential in its way than his predecessors. Patricia Hollis has summarized the main thrust of this radicalism as being based on a critique of 'old corruption' (1970). This analysis concentrated on the abuse of power by politicians and the abuse of working people. The 'older rhetoric' highlighted the corruption at the heart of the political system and essentially expressed the problems of society in terms of the inadequacies of powerful and wealthy individuals. The rhetoric of the 'old corruption' was shared by middle class and working-class radicals of the time and drew on folk memory and the oral tradition of the Free Born Englishman established in the wake of the Seventeenth-Century English Revolution. Harrison indicates that after the impact of the French Revolution on popular political aspirations and in the maelstrom of industrialization, it was no surprise that the first champion of popular rights should be articulated in such a 'yeomanly' figure as Cobbett for it was precisely the values of the rural artisan and traditional culture, in its broadest definition as a whole way of life, that the actions of a new mercantile and political elite seemed to be threatening (Harrison, 1974: 43). Nor, for the same reasons, is it any surprise that the voice which articulated this 'older rhetoric' should do so in a way which called on established traditions of a common English identity. Williams writes that what the nineteenth century brought was, with Cobbett, 'a new kind of campaigning political journalism' (Williams, 1978: 47). He returned to the tradition of the political essay but used it to provide an entirely new point of attack on privilege from the unshakeable perspective of empathy with the underdog in desperately hard economic times:

> I, as far as I am convinced, am quite willing to trust to the talent, the justice and the loyalty of the great mass of the people . . . I am quite willing to make *common cause* with them, *to be one of them.* (*Cobbett's Political Register* (*CPR*), No. 31, 24 April 1819)

For Cobbett just as for Paine, '*truth* in *clear language*' (*CPR*, No. 18, 1810: October 10) was the first priority of the radical author and it was a language which made full use of direct address to the people of its sympathy as well as in its hostility, providing a 'blunt simplicity of appeal to the masses' (Herd, 1952: 103) which was the chief characteristic of his writing:

> Will nothing, oh people of England, short of destruction itself, convince you that you are on the road to destruction? Will you, in spite of the awful admonition of events, in spite of experimental conviction, in spite of truths that you acknowledge, still listen to the falsehoods of your deceivers? (*CPR*, No. 9, 1 March 1806)

Indeed, this direct address and the presumed bond of solidarity which flowed from it formed a central part of the structuring of his political thought. Thompson goes so far as to claim that 'Cobbett's thought was not a system but a *relationship*' with his audience (1967: 758). This was expressed as a practical engagement with the people he met on his travels throughout the land and in his ability to embrace the issues they raised with him in straightforward language. His reference to his 'readers or hearers' in his *Political Register* shows how the reading of unstampeds was above all an activity that working-class persons performed as members of a newly demotic public sphere (Wickwar, 1928: 54). He began to conflate discussions of class and language and encouraged readers to see that limitations on the abilities of people to engage in debate about politics in everyday language was an integral part of a social system which he was calling upon them to change (Smith, 1984: 110).

Much of the appeal of Cobbett's writing lay in the ways he drew upon a common cultural archive for his narratives of an older, more harmonious England; a nation more at peace with itself and one which could demonstrate more patriotic pride in its singularity and achievements particularly in its rural idylls as '. . . an accumulated vocabulary of motifs, tropes, and epithets . . . a sustained relationship to other forms of rural representation' (Helsinger, 1997: 104–105). These narratives and their symbolic reference points would have been familiar to most of the recently urbanized population as well as to the rural population itself. Many of the narratives of injustice for which Cobbett became famous, drew on the patterns of broadsheets and ballads and appealed to an already receptive audience because they connected with the real life experiences of many of his readers and provided a reassuring reformulation of a common store of folk memories. One of the most important areas for this process of normative integration was in the discourse of the nation where Cobbett democratized historical vocabulary by defining the nation as '*the whole of the people*' (Dyck, 1992: 127) confirming that Cobbett himself, even in his radical phase, remained essentially a patriot. Despite the fact that he embodied the early-century paradigm of the popular journalist as an opinionated, authoritative voice of the people, he nevertheless expressed a force for cohesion in British society based around the concept of a readership of printed matter as a national community with interests in common. Newspapers had an important role in extending a sense of imagined continuity across geographical space as a national community (Anderson, 1986) which was to have implications for the way in which popular periodical discourse came to be articulated throughout the century.

Cobbett was able to widen his readership, not only because he employed a vernacular which attempted to popularize politics so that the ordinary people could make sense of the dramatic changes of early-nineteenth-century England, but also because he wrote in an idiom which drew clearly on the traditions and speech patterns of popular culture. His was a rhetoric which attempted and succeeded in bridging the traditional and the radical and sought to bring that new community together across a range of common interests. To this end, his writing was full of the interruptions, ejaculations, emphases and conveyed the strength of his feeling on particular topics by capital letters, exclamation and question marks, breaking:

> the usual decorum (that is, among the middle and upper classes) of
> formal spoken or written English . . . the flow of the text is broken

> up by what is heard as the abrupt rise and fall of emphatically inflected speech and felt as the jerks and stabs of an equally emphatic body language. (Helsinger, 1997: 133)

He understood that the common people had become politically aware to the extent that they could no longer simply be preached at and that in order to incorporate their support for resistance to the corruption in English society, he had to find a voice with which they could become identified. He was emphatic in not talking down to this readership but, on the contrary, in highlighting its accumulated knowledge gained in the lived experience of the times. Writing of the Bishop of Landoff's claim that Paine's *Age of Reason* constituted an act of blasphemy, Cobbett opined:

> However, I am of the opinion that your Lordship is very much deceived in supposing the People, or the vulgar, as you please to call them, *to be incapable of comprehending argument* . . . The People do not at all relish little simple tales. Neither do they delight in declamatory language, or in loose assertion; their minds have, within the last ten years, undergone a very great revolution. (*CPR*, No. 21, 27 January 1820)

Cobbett was a traditionalist as well as a populist. He was a patriot as well as being deeply resentful of the appropriation of the discourse of patriotism by forces with which he disagreed. He was a paternalist whose vision of rural self-sufficiency sat ill at ease with the industrializing pressures of the day. He was radical to an extent but lacked the analytical insight which would have enabled him to transcend the restrictions of the 'old rhetoric' yet Cobbett's rhetoric provided a reservoir for political journalism in the years to come whose cadences and bluntness can certainly be detected in contemporary popular journalism.

Thomas Wooler: Parody and the popular

A very different contribution to the radical press from the sustained and serious critical polemic of Cobbett and the Hunts came in Wooler's *Black Dwarf* (*BD*). The *Black Dwarf* 1817–1824 started as a 4 pence weekly publication. By 1819 it had gained such notoriety that Castelreagh, the Foreign Secretary, announced in Parliament that Wooler had become the 'fugleman of the Radicals' and that his *Black Dwarf* could be found in northern mining areas, 'in the hatcrown of almost every pitman you meet' (Wickwar, 1928: 57).

The *Black Dwarf* was a provocative contribution to the radical newspaper tradition, not only in its content but more especially in its style. It contained a strong blend of satire, parody and humorous intervention in support of Reform and the interests of the labouring classes. Drawing on the popular culture of the working poor, poetry, ballads, songs were all published in support of radical ideas and the culture they supported. It blended with the oral nature of popular culture in its use of reported speeches, quotations, questions, answers and parodies. His satire remained very much within the 'old corruption' school – iconoclastic and populist, developing a style of anti-authoritarianism with a strong contemporary flavour. It offered little in explicit analysis but it pro-vided a style which went beyond reporting and set the tone for political debate among a new audience, a tone which was based on the 'expanded use of public satire . . .' (Hendrix, 1976: 128). Its motto made this explicit:

> Satire's my weapon; but I'm too discreet,
> *To run a-muck and tilt at all I meet:*
> POPE

Although it announced itself in this motto as following in the tradition of the satirical model of Pope's imitation of Horace's satires, Wooler was not interested in some polite critique of the foibles of society and indeed did tilt at most everything that he met. The paper's subtitle, the 'Address to the Unrepresented Part of the Community' makes clear both the constituency his paper was aimed at, as well as stressing the fact that in order to change society, this community had to become more actively aware of their current situation:

> . . . You are *something*, you are indeed; and although few dare tell you what you are, you must perceive yourselves to be '*slaves, on whose chains are inscribed the words liberty and freedom!'* SLAVES? Englishmen Slaves? You are startled, and well you may be, but it should be at your *condition*, and not at the proclamation of it. Look around you. Do, I beseech you, make use of your eyes. (*BD*: Vol. 2, No. 27, 8 July 1818)

As in the example above, Wooler often employed devices based on an approximation of oral patterns in order to appeal to readers and, no doubt, listeners who would have had the paper read to them by a reader drawing upon all its visual clues for intended delivery. Yet despite its evident service to the radical movement encapsulated in its informa-tional content, the most significant aspect of Wooler's project was the way in which he used his paper to play humorously with the conven-tional forms of the newspaper itself. The novelty of the *Black Dwarf*'s humorous engagement with politics from a radical stance was that it highlighted the instability of established (and the Establishment's) forms of the newspaper as a forum for public information. In doing so, it also made the most of the instability of contemporary readerships. Klancher has observed that during these years it was the English Romantics, sensing the turbulence of these times, who first became radically uncertain of their readership and faced the task Wordsworth referred to as '*creating* the taste' by which the writer is comprehended (Klancher, 1987: 3). At this moment, the English reading public was experiencing the social and demographic turmoil of the industrial revolution as a new social and political consciousness was being created among the working class. Wooler exploited this to the full in providing a complex range of voices and textual experiments to articulate that sense of change and uncertainty. Even his protagonist, the Black Dwarf himself, was a symbol of mutability and radical unpredictability of shape and form. He is described in the first edition by Wooler as 'secure from his invisibility, and dangerous from his power of division, (for like the polypus, he can divide and redivide himself, and each division remain a perfect animal)' (*BD*: Vol. 1, No. 1, 29 January 1817).

The instability of the 'polymorph' is reflected in the highly volatile mixture of voices (heteroglossia) which Wooler uses to destabilize and critique the ruling classes and their institutions and customs. One of the chief targets of his comic strategies is the established newspaper form which was continuing on its own way towards an economically and politically acceptable truce with the status quo. Bakhtin has stressed the importance of orientating one's language in opposition to the dominant discourse of the time, highlighting the dynamic nature of this process:

> Language is not a neutral medium that passes freely and easily into the private property of the speaker's intentions; it is populated – overpopulated – with the intentions of others. . . . Consciousness finds itself inevitably facing the necessity of – *having to choose a language*. With each literary-verbal performance, consciousness must actively orient itself amidst heteroglossia, it must move in and occupy a position for itself within it, it chooses in other words, a 'language'. (1996: 294–295)

Wooler uses this multiplicity of language and voice to demonstrate the complexity of choice within which his readers were being invited to take their place. The Black Dwarf, the Yellow Bonze, the Green Goblin, the Black Neb and the Blue Devil all provide different voices and perspectives within which Wooler can confront and ridicule the corruption of the status quo. This variety of voices, a literal heteroglossia, allows Wooler to take up a whole spectrum of satirical and parodic positions which would have been closed to the more traditional and literal writing of Cobbett or Paine. Wooler was also adamant that the variety of textual voices had to be complemented by genuine dialogue among his readers:

> It is only in communion with his fellows, that man rises to the full importance of his being . . . He, who only reads in his closet, may be very well informed, and yet very useless . . . To be important, men must meet each other, unite their knowledge and their powers, compare their sentiments, weigh together the force of opposite statements – and draw the pure gold of truth from the dross of the inferior ore with which it is generally combined. (*BD*: Vol. 3, No. 3, January 1819)

Wooler deployed a wide range of journalism's repertoire for comic/ disruptive effect 'reporting' 'foreign correspondents' 'political discourse', 'reports of trials', 'poetry' and 'readers' letters' were all used to destabilize and force reflection on the purpose of journalism and its relationship to those in power. However, ultimately, even the heroic efforts of Wooler to invigorate the cause of reform were exhausted by the declining fortune of radical papers in the wake of increased taxation and surveillance of the radical press after 1819 (Wood, 1994: 13). He is writing from an apparent trough of despondency in the last copy of his paper in 1824 in his 'Final Address':

> In ceasing his political labours, the Black Dwarf has to regret one mistake, and that a serious one. He commenced writing under the idea that there was a PUBLIC in Britain, and that public devotedly attached to the cause of parliamentary reform. This, it is but candid to admit, was an error. (*BD*: Vol. 12, No. 21, December 1824)

The Six Acts: Reaction and reconfiguration

In 1819 the introduction by Parliament of the 'Six Acts' severely curtailed the activities of the radical press. They included a Blasphemous and Seditious Libels Act and also made it necessary for bonds of £200– £300 to be paid over to the authorities in surety before a paper could be published, in order to ensure that the press was in the hands of respectable, politically responsible owners. This legislation, combined with an improvement in economic conditions and the execution of the Cato Street conspirators, ensured the decline of overt political radicalism in the short term (McCalman, 1998: 181).

Complementary to this suppression, the radical popular press was rapidly incorporated and eventually transformed, through the regular publication of periodicals of sensational entertainment. The *Terrific Register*, started in 1821, with woodcuts and stories of 'Crimes, Judgements, Providences and Calamities', provided little change from popular reading of centuries past in the almanacs, broadsides and ballads which had been eschewed by the respectable press as a marketable commodity for so long. Its difference lay in its regular publication. In addition, there was the economically astute construction of the popular Sunday press as entertainment papers such as *Bell's Weekly Messenger* began publication from 1822. Sunday papers were ideal for the workers who could not afford the price of the daily newspapers and who because of the long hours and the lack of artificial evening light in their accommodation were unable to read apart from on a Sunday, their day of rest.

In addition to legislative measures and market alternatives, there were increased efforts to provide a style of popular periodical which might combine an appeal to working people with a less radical component. The Society for the Diffusion of Useful Knowledge was founded in 1826 to help in the creation of a more content worker. From 1827 this was complemented by a *Library of Useful Knowledge* as a fortnightly collection of pieces on a range of topics from Greek literature to popular science. The contents and aspirations of such publications were patronizing and largely irrelevant to their targeted readers as was highlighted by the *Westminster Review* of April 1831. To combat such criticisms, in 1832 Charles Knight launched the *Penny Magazine* in an attempt to broaden the work of the Society for the Diffusion of Useful Knowledge (SDUK) and reach the lower orders with useful knowledge and thereby rescue them from sedition and political corruption. This fulfilled the ambition he had expressed in the *London Magazine* of April 1828 that working people having been taught to read and consequently to think had loosed a new power in society and this 'could not be stopped although it might be given direction' (Harrison, 1974: 101). Circulation reached 200,000 but despite this success, the SDUK was dissolved, in 1846, shortly after the discontinuation of the *Penny Magazine* in 1845 with its considered work done and its objectives achieved (Jones, 1996: 107). A complementary reason for this was no doubt that a more genuinely popular form of popular periodical and the Sunday newspaper had started to take their place, and most importantly for the government, one divested of genuinely radical politics.

The second phase of unstamped newspapers

It has been said that in the nineteenth century, 'the image of the newspaper as a harbinger, or indeed the active agent, of change exerted a powerful hold over the contemporary imagination' (Jones, 1996: xi). This had much to do with the increasing ability of many newspapers to match their language and content to the interests of particular classes of people, particularly those actively seeking social change. A second wave of radical, unstamped periodicals responded to further political and economic convulsions in the 1830s. These working-class unstampeds may be divided into three main ideological trends: *pragmatic*, *utopian* and *confrontational* (Chalaby, 1998: 19) and all varieties differed from earlier radical journals in that they gave news, in the government definition of the word, as they reported and commented on each stage in the Reform Bill struggle (Harrison, 1974: 81). Yet it was in the language of the confrontational newspapers where we most clearly see the analysis of a 'new rhetoric' (Hollis, 1970) which aimed to transcend individual articulations of grievances to be found in 'old corruption' analyses and to provide a proto-socialist analysis of the position of working people within the economic system of industrial capitalism and particularly within the structures of property ownership. This rhetoric contributed to an emergent understanding of social class by going beyond simplistic dichotomies of virtuous working people and the wicked rich in attempting to develop an understanding of the systemic causes of popular discontent. Their titles declared their intent: *The Crisis, The Prompter, The Destructive, The Republican, The Working Man's Friend.* The middle class radicals were on the point of inheriting the benefits of the Reform Act of 1832 but the confrontational working class radicals looked to their press as an instrument to militate for deeper political and economic changes. These unstamped newspapers raised the political awareness of the dominated classes by using language and recurrent themes which drew upon the political experience of these readers: 'by putting feelings into words, by expressing grievances, by proposing political modes of actions and economic solutions, by giving hope and by organizing the political activities and political life as a whole of the working classes' (Chalaby, 1998: 18–19).

Hetherington's *Penny Papers for the People* from 1 October 1830 was closely associated from the start with the National Union of the Working Classes and was soon renamed the *Poor Man's Guardian* (*PMG*). Its opening editorial declared:

> It is the cause of the *rabble* we advocate, the poor, the suffering, the industrious, the productive classes . . . We will teach this rabble their power – we will teach them that they are your master, instead of being your slaves.

The *Poor Man's Guardian* was notable for the hundreds of letters (Harrison, 1974: 83) which helped establish a communicative channel between paper and readers at the same time as its editors sought to elaborate a radical social and political critique. A perfect illustration of its attempt to supplement this communicative strategy by deploying a new rhetoric focused on the structural inequalities within social practice, comes from a colleague and supporter of Hetherington's political analysis, Bronterre O'Brien, popularizing the thought of contemporary economic analyst, Hodgskin, writing in a passage typical of this new analytical style:

> Now, since all wealth is the produce of industry, and as the privileged fraction produce nothing themselves, it is plain that they must live on the labours of the rest. But how is this to be done, since every body thinks it enough to work for himself? It is done partly by fraud and partly by force. The 'property' people having all the law-making to themselves, make and maintain fraudulent institutions, by which they contrive (under false pretences) to transfer the wealth of the producers to themselves. (*PMG*, 26 June 1834)

O'Brien's *Destructive* confronted the liberal intentions of the SDUK and suggested that the provision of provocative information liable to overthrow the system should be the purpose of his paper on 7 June 1834:

> Some simpletons talk of knowledge as rendering the working classes more obedient, more dutiful . . . But such knowledge is trash; the only knowledge which is of any service to the working people is that which makes them more dissatisfied and makes them worse slaves. This is the knowledge we shall give them.

Such papers were in the process of creating a new class identity and despite their short-lived careers, they were laying the foundations for the newspapers of the Chartist movement and also, in many ways, providing further sophistication to the tradition and appeal of radical journalism. However, their radical intent needs to be understood in a broader context. These unstamped newspapers made money and provided the platform for the development of a popular press which had a role in defining the printed manifestation of the interests of the working classes of Britain. It was, in fact, their commercial success which encouraged the development of a particular style of popular press from the Chartist movement onwards. James has observed the paradox of this incorporation of the popular into a commercial paradigm: 'The Radical press was . . . forced out by the popularity of the very cheap literature it had helped to establish' (James, 1976: 36). Within the logic of a liberal print economy, any popular press which restricted itself to a purely political role would ultimately lose out against a more commercially orientated popularity. The radical press, even as it became increasingly commercialized, lost its potential to rival the increasingly broad appeal of the Sunday and later daily popular press within such a commercial environment. If a paper claimed to speak for the people, this could only be legitimated if in fact it had a wide enough circulation to interest advertisers. Increasingly, the newspapers able to achieve such circulations did so through developing broader approaches than the more narrowly, didactically popular-political. They returned in many ways to previous patterns of popular print culture which had already become established as having a wide general appeal. They included a diverse range of content including sensation and the serialization of novels in their efforts to capture the broadest coalition of popular taste although one subjugated to an overarching profit motive. As if to confirm this trend, Hetherington consequently altered his approach to content in his publication, the *Destructive*, which in June 1834 proclaimed that it would:

> ... henceforward be a repository of all the gems and treasures, and fun and frolic and 'news and occurrences' of the week. It shall abound in Police Intelligences, in Murders, Rapes, Suicides, Burnings, Maimings, Theatricals, Races, Pugilism, and all manner of moving 'accidents by flood and field'. In short it will be stuffed with every sort of devilment that will make it sell.

Heatherington, and more successfully, Cleave, in his *Weekly Police Gazette* (1834) were able to bring together aspects of the radical opinion of the Unstamped and the profitability of their formats at a price which would challenge the supremacy, on the one hand, of the street literature and peddled broadsides and, on the other, the comfortable superiority of the middle-class papers and the class these represented. To an extent, the new popular papers were able to claim a growing political legitimacy, despite their sometimes ambivalent intentions, simply on the strength of their widespread readership which took them beyond the reach of a social minority. As soon as the popular press was able to perfect this formula, it would appear that its democratic credentials, albeit limited in scope, were established. Hollis concludes that ultimately the new radicals failed to replace the older rhetoric with the new (Hollis, 1970: vii). The emerging working class could not be reduced to one function or one aspiration. A popular press henceforth had to allow for a more dialogic interplay between the genres of information and entertainment and the economic environment created pressure for such a resolution to be found. James argues that it was to a large extent radical journalism which cemented the disparate experiences and practices of the working classes into a sense of class solidarity while acknowledging that there was, even within this formation a divide between those who wanted to read for entertainment and those who wanted to read as a political activity (James, 1976: 22). Clearly, anything which was able to cross between these modes of appeal could begin to draw maximum commercial returns from a considerable reading public.

Market compromises: Popular tastes

There were two quite distinct responses to the political radicalism of the unstamped, the respectable and the scurrilous. The respectable publications included *Chamber's Edinburgh Journal, Penny Magazine of the Society for the Diffusion of Useful Knowledge* and *The Saturday Magazine* all published in 1832 and all seeking to supply the demand for instruction and entertainment evinced by the success of the Sunday papers but in more wholesome ways. Despite their initial success, it was the scurrilous variety which were to have the more lasting and influential popular appeal in terms of its impact upon the parameters of the language of the popular newspaper, and ultimately on the newspaper in general.

The bawdy and the politically subversive had long shared a network of profitable illegality (McCalman, 1998) so it was no surprise that they came to blend their approaches to enhance their popular appeal. Benbow exploited older traditions of scandal and aristocratic corruption (Darnton, 1996) to produce his *Rambler's Magazine* of 1822. He expanded the scope of his publication to provide more of general appeal to the working classes and this revised agenda extended from sport and criminal trials to popular literature and radical politics. The sexual element of Benbow's publication was commercially moderated in 1833 by Penney, a stationer by trade, who was confident enough of the market to bring out his broadsheet *People's Police Gazette*. It was filled with police news and court reports and quickly achieved a circulation of 20,000 (Harrison, 1974: 94). Following suit, from 1834, two of the unstamped publishers produced broadsheets of their own Hetherington's *Twopenny Dispatch* and Cleave's *Weekly Police Gazette* which was to have an impact on the development of crime content in popular daily newspapers in the United States. McCalman (1998: 236) argues that it is in the blend of the language of shocking exposé of the sexual corruption of the upper classes with the equally shocking political corruption of politicians that these publications began to refashion the tastes of the English working-class reader from a political and class-conscious phase of the 1820s and 1830s to a more escapist, insubordinate yet apolitical form by the 1870s. The Sunday weekly newspapers were to provide the melting pot in which the new culture would be born out of the old.

The voice of provincial radicalism

Provincial newspapers also continued to develop dialogues with their readers and acted as disseminators of reformist opinion on a local level

73

(Read, 1961: 62). The *Manchester Guardian* launched on Saturday, 5 May 1821, modelled on provincial middle-class reform newspapers such as the *Leeds Mercury* and the *Liverpool Mercury* carried editorial articles and reports from public meetings from the start. The political theory of Jeremy Bentham, for example, was accepted in its most democratic form:

> we maintain, that in forming our opinion with respect to parliamentary reform, all we have to do, is to ascertain whether it is for the advantage of the people ('The universal interest', as Bentham well designates them), that it should take place. Its effects, either upon the king or the house of peers, are matters of merely secondary importance. (*Manchester Guardian,* 7 September 1822)

During the Reform Bill crisis, Harland, its chief reporter, took down details which according to Read (1961): 'retained all the vigour, and colour of the speeches . . . first person reporting such as had rarely been known before in the provincial press: vigorous language authentically recorded':

> I have no language adequate to express the dread I feel of their rejecting it – I have no nerve to reflect upon the consequences of such a course – and sure I am that if they do reject it, not only will their own order be endangered, but everything that is valuable in this fine country. Gentlemen, I call upon you, as you value your families, as you value your friends, as you wish to retain your property, and, above all, as you love your country, to use all the influences you possess (and every man does possess influence) to endeavour to carry this great measure which I cannot but denominate the charter of your rights. (*Manchester Guardian,* 24 September 1831)

To counter the sell-out of the working classes in the Reform Act of 1832, Chartism was born. The six points of the Charter, published in May 1838 could be summarized as: universal [male] suffrage, annual parliaments, voting by ballot, the creation of equal electoral districts, the abolition of property qualification for voting, the payment of members of parliament. The vitality of the language of political debate was widely disseminated by the provincial press, especially when it became in certain cities allied to the cause of the Chartist movement. In the *Chartist*, a full account is provided of a London meeting complete with the interventions of the audience for added effect and one senses, as an amplification of the approval of the readership:

> POOR LAW AMENDMENT ACT
>
> On Monday a public meeting convened by the National Anti-Poor Law Association, was held at the Freemasons' Tavern, Great

Queen-street, Lincoln's Inn-fields, for the purpose of deliberating upon the means to be adopted to remedy the evils of the Poor Law Amendment Act . . .

The noble CHAIRMAN, in opening the business of the day, said the business they had to consider was whether the people would continue to tolerate, without the strongest resistance, the arbitrary power of the three directors of Somerset House, who would not have been endured by our forefathers – a power unconstitutional in its principle, and cruel and oppressive in its operation – (Cheers.) Another question for their consideration was whether they would preserve that which they had enjoyed for centuries and that which they had greatly prized – the right of self-government – (Cheer)- a right and principle which, as Englishmen, was dear to them, that of expending their own money, and in a way which they thought would most conduce to the welfare of their poorer neighbours – (Cheers) . . . and would ask them whether or not they were willing . . . that the relief should be dispensed according to the rules, orders, and regulations of three despots at Somerset House? (Cheers and cries of 'No'.). (The *Chartist,* Sunday, 30 June 1839)

The *Northern Star:* A principled political voice

Provincial engagement with radical politics reaches its zenith in the publication of the *Northern Star* (1837–1852) in Leeds. It was identifiably a newspaper with all the range and variety that this had come to represent; yet it provided, in addition, a steady and coherent expression of the principles of the Chartist cause. Its opening number of *Northern Star* 18 November 1837 locates it firmly in opposition to the mainstream press:

> The silence of the Press upon all subjects connected with the movement-party has been pointed and obvious; and, amongst others who have anxiously endeavoured to serve the public cause, I have met with marked indifference, and even insult, where it could be safely hazarded . . . The power of the press is acknowledged upon all hands, and rather than oppose it, I have preferred to arm myself with it.

Epstein has commented that in fusing in his newspaper the functions of 'the powers of the press with those of the platform' (Epstein, 1976: 51), Fergus O'Connor, the self-styled People's Champion, was continuing the tradition of William Cobbett. The tone of this organ was a written version of the public assembly. It represented a didactic form of political leadership aimed at bridging the gap between an oral and a written political culture which clearly aimed to lead the people through the complexities of contemporary politics with a rhetoric which claimed to emanate from the people themselves but was, in fact, that of their self-appointed champion, O'Connor. This aim was encapsulated in its editor's word from 1842:

> I set myself, therefore, to see the people in possession of an organ which, trumpet-tongued, might speak their will, and utter their complaint. (*Northern Star*, 19 November 1842: 2)

Epstein observes that the language of the paper was 'stridently class-conscious . . . the razor-sharp rhetoric of class war' (Epstein, 1976: 71). The *Star* could also claim the essential popular element of wide appeal and therefore profitability, albeit within a particular social class, claiming almost half a million readers by the end of the 1830s. However, its profits were ploughed back into agitation and the support of political causes supported by the newspaper and involving the struggles of working people. Certain techniques of the popular cheap press were adopted such as woodcuts and steel-engraved portraits of heroes of the Chartist movement while O'Connor also adapted to popular tastes by an anecdotal style in his weekly letters which he wrote with the keen ear for oral delivery of a skilled public orator practised in addressing popular audiences in public places. O'Connor retained what Thompson has called the Wilkesite tradition of gentlemanly leadership to which the democratic movement still deferred (Thompson, 1967: 682) which would leave his paper open to criticism of speaking down to its readership. Such a restrictive voice would eventually drive readership to a more commercially oriented heteroglossia. Vincent points out this process when he writes that the *Northern Star* was:

> . . . too dependent on the position of its proprietor to escape the negative aspects of the personalisation of address which had been so characteristic of the working-class political papers. O'Connor's 'MY Dear Friends . . . had become "My Dear Children"' by the time of the Third Petition in 1848. (Vincent, 1993: 251)

Conclusion

Chalaby (1998: 16–18) has argued against using the term 'journalists' to describe these writers, preferring instead the word 'publicists' and although there is a certain analytical correctness about the distinction between their differing styles and functions, the publications of the early and mid-nineteenth century did feed into developments within language which helped to shape the language of newspapers for popular audiences. These periodicals served to open up the complexities of social life beyond the interests of a narrowly politicized bourgeois class and began the process of articulating the lives, passions and politics of ordinary working people. The radical press of the early nineteenth century performed a dual function by representing the people as well as keeping them informed about matters in their interest and it did both of these in a language which was close to their own spoken idiom. These publications demonstrate how demotic language was able to challenge the bourgeois hegemony within public communication opening up a rival public sphere (Eley, 1992). Gilmartin has identified the rich over-determination in the composition of the public sphere represented by the nineteenth-century radical press:

> Its formal development must be understood in relation to the linked histories of press restriction, print technology, the economics of publishing, radical rhetoric and organization, and popular reading habits. (Gilmartin, 1996: 75)

This point echoes the observation made earlier in the book that the products and practices of newspaper language have always been in a struggle for dominance with other rival discourses and definitions. Williams (1978) insists that journalism should not be narrated from the standpoint of what it became as if that were somehow inevitable and historically neutral. Newspapers and their language were in a continuous process of formation against a whole range of competing political, cultural and textual practices.

4 Shaping the social market

Introduction

The nineteenth century saw several profound changes to the language of newspapers. These took place in the context of the consolidation of the political influence and economic stature of the *Times*; the subsequent development of newspapers to rival this dominance which sought to discover alternative ways of reaching an affluent middle class; the generation of a market for weekly newspapers aimed at a working-class readership; the post-telegraph shift in the flow and organization of language within newspaper institutions. Early changes in the mid-century were partly driven by an extension in the franchise which allowed a widening section of the public to vote and partly by an increasing commercialization which encouraged a marketing of newspapers for much more explicit and socially based readerships than had previously been available. The first electoral change came with the Reform Act of 1832. Its effect was to increase the numbers of propertied middle-class voters and these immediately became a target of newspapers directed towards a readership freshly interested in parliamentary proceedings as well as commerce and general news. The diversifying social base of newspaper readerships were provided for by new developments throughout the century such as the illustrated weeklies, Sunday papers, political and cultural quarterlies and later, more popular-based monthlies, daily evening newspapers and the eventual targeting of the lower middle classes. These were all accompanied by the pursuit of a variety of languages of identification aimed at establishing commercially viable print communities.

The market orientation of newspapers

It was after the final lifting of taxes on newspapers in 1855 that the style and content of the newspaper began to consistently address the social specifics of its readers within a liberal market economy. Politicians were proved correct that newspapers would subsequently be increasingly accountable to the views of the respectable classes of society through the market and would therefore be less politically partisan because of their dependence on the business of advertisers and the desire of readers for reliable and impartial information. The market mood became attuned to encourage broadly liberal newspapers after 1855 (Curran, 1978). These provided liberal hegemonic positions broadly favourable to the political status quo and as a consequence were commercially attractive in their broad-based appeal. They further extended this appeal with a corresponding miscellany in content which was becoming the dominant pattern within newspapers. This matched a particularly influential philosophical discourse of the time which asserted a preference for a free market of ideas determined within a competitive economic market (Mill, 1989: 19–55).

The word 'journalism' entered the English language via an article in the *Westminster Review* (1833) and Campbell (2000) provides a persuasive explanation that this neologism signalled an attempt to delineate a style of writing which narrowed down previously existing divisions between high culture and popular culture. Indeed, she claims that journalism played a prominent part in the formation of the language of modernity since the term 'journalism' was introduced in order to account for the characteristic tensions which newspapers brought into the public arena, as they located their appeal between elite and popular knowledge. From this moment onwards, the momentum of the language of newspapers was driven inexorably by a process of popularization. By popularization, we mean the production of news which was aimed at larger and larger numbers of readers and which claimed to espouse their political and social interests. It was a process which also shifted from the ambition of providing enlightenment for a specific readership to one of imagining and therefore representing that readership (Hampton, 2004). This led to extensive experimentation with editorial style and attempts to create distinctive identities for newspapers as each sought to establish a regular readership within an increasingly competitive environment. These editorial identities provided a much broader range than those fostered in the late eighteenth century.

While daily newspapers increased their appeal to middle-class audiences, Sunday newspapers took up the mantle of being representatives of the working classes with a judicious blend of sensation, entertainment and radical perspectives on the interests of the working classes, although securely harnessed within a commercially acceptable format. Both these forms of newspaper developed their own, distinct styles of writing but it would be the popular end of the market which, as it tried to find ways of appealing to a more generalist and less explicitly politicized readership, would move the style of journalism towards what we have come to know as its dominant style. The weekly Sunday newspapers, with their huge popular readerships, were to provide the driving momentum of journalism through their increasing harmonization of miscellany, entertainment, melodramatic narrative and contemporary news.

From the early Victorian period, with newspapers more accepted within the social and political mainstream as commercial products, addressed to general rather than politically motivated readers, the writing of journalists started to become more distinguishable from other forms of literary output. According to (Elliott, 1978) the journalist started the long climb towards political, if not social, respectability in the nineteenth century. This, however, was a slow process over the course of the nineteenth century (Brake, 1994), and leading politicians and contemporary philosophers contributed to, as well as edited, newspapers and periodicals. This distinction was gradually eroded as the role of journalists became more accepted as a specialist component in the negotiation of social and political trends to expanding readerships. This necessitated the evolution of various styles of language driven by the growing specialization within newspapers as editorials, feature articles, background commentaries, the report from various specialists covering sporting events, politics and the court started to drift apart stylistically after 1855.

The social orientation of newspapers to different markets meant that newspapers developed strategies within their language to bring various constituents within one discursive pattern. Political reports, general news, low-life crime, scandal, advertising and editorials, to name but a few of the varieties contained in the early Victorian press, needed to be framed within a unified editorial approach determined by specific market appeal. Earlier, both radical and liberal newspapers and periodicals had tended towards a political public and a drawing together of publics as homogenous groupings motivated in particular by issues such as reliability of commercial information, accurate political reporting, the extension of the franchise and the rights of working people. From 1855, their language was increasingly designed to appeal to specific parts of a commercial market identifiable by leisure, class, profession and income. The changes in newspapers from having a predominantly political function to a commercial one were dramatically accelerated by the lifting of taxes on newspapers in 1855. These developments formed part of what has been termed, 'the transition from a public to a journalistic discourse' (Chalaby, 1998: 66). Chalaby goes on to claim that from this point, 'journalism can be considered as the commodified form of public discourse'.

It has been remarked that the newspaper press moved into the centre of British life during the course of the nineteenth century (Jones, 1996: xi) and was set to dominate over the sermon and the public meeting as a generalized disseminator of information and opinion by the end of the century. As such, it was also a prime social barometer and the language of these newspapers came increasingly to act as a key element in social differentiation. One of the consequences flowing from the increasingly commercialized social market for newspapers was that readerships were being defined according to: '. . . broad bands of class stratification . . .' (Lee, 1976: 19). In political discussions of how newspapers engaged with their readers, Hampton argues that two analytically distinct approaches predominated: 'educational', a commitment to trying to 'influence' readers of the truth or common good and a contrasting 'representative' approach by newspapers reflecting the already-existing opinions and tastes of readers (Hampton, 2001: 214). As a complement to the break in discursive patternings identified above (Chalaby, 1998), post 1855, this shift from 'educational' to 'representative' is the second decisive discursive shift within the nineteenth-century newspaper's language.

The fourth estate as political legitimation

Journalism's rise to a level of political and social legitimacy was based on the establishment of its profitable commercial status which enabled newspapers to become independent of political control. Their journalism was often hailed as a Fourth Estate although this was neither a consistent nor absolutely clear set of practices. The claim to constitute a Fourth Estate was however a fundamental aspect to the discursive formation of journalism. The language of newspapers becomes structured as a discourse in Foucault's terms (1974) as it provides an expression of the dominant values in society while allowing powerful new forms of social identification through those values. As we have seen in the introductory chapter in this book, the legitimation of journalism was able to present itself as a powerful form of control over the political establishment, a Fourth Estate of the realm, while establishing itself as an equally powerful form of social control on behalf of commercial self-interest. In the mid-nineteenth century, newspapers in particular had already become too dependent on advertising and economic stability to want to seriously consider challenging the political establishment, yet journalism was able through its self-claimed status as Fourth Estate to provide an important rhetorical bridge between the economic interests of the newspapers and the self-interest of the newly enfranchised British middle classes. Both sets of activities, middle-class involvement in politics and the establishment of profitable and independent newspapers, claimed legitimacy through this connection and through it forged one of the most historically resilient claims of newspaper journalism. Much of the 'ideological baggage' (Boyce, 1978: 19) of the Fourth Estate becomes attached to journalism's descriptions and expectations of itself from this point. Jones argues that it retained a powerful role within journalism throughout the nineteenth century (Jones, 1996: 12–13). A good example of this comes from the *Times*' leader writer, Reeve, outlining the trajectory of politically interventionist journalism from Junius to the mid-Victorian era:

> Junius . . . set the example of that union of accurate and secret political information, consummate ability, daring liberty, and pungent and racy style, which has ever since distinguished the highest organs of the newspaper press. (Reeve, 1855: 472)

The *Times*: A paradigm of political influence

The discourse of the Fourth Estate was founded within a journalistic landscape which had been largely cleared of alternatives which were not market-based. The journalism which flourished was unequivocally a branch of commerce and this was reinforced by the triple pressures of technology, capital and distribution. Technological innovations came at a cost and newspaper ownership became restricted to those who could invest in equipment and property as well as coordinate the logistical organization required to exploit the growing railway network as a distribution channel. With increasing capitalization came the need to provide more specialist roles within a newspaper as the jobs of reporters, printers, advertising sales people, editors and specialist correspondents became demarcated and formalized. To support such changes in the structure of newspapers, the requirements for large sums of capital investment meant a greater dependence than ever on circulation combined with advertising revenue. The *Times* was the paper which established the most dominant early form of this market-orientated independent journalism.

Already successful as part of the Walters' publishing business, it was under the editorship of Thomas Barnes (1817–1841) that it started its move to its position of dominance. Under Barnes, it 'was vastly improved as a newspaper, in the sense of a collector and retailer of information' (Fox-Bourne, 1998, Vol. 2: 110). He ensured that it drew on an extensive range of public opinion through a nationwide network of correspondents and was able to channel this astutely into leading articles which took on impressive resonance as reflections of elite opinion among the bourgeoisie. This network was extended to international sources to supplement information from domestic informants in order to turn the newspaper into a much more complete purveyor and processor of news and one which was increasingly able to reflect critically and with authority upon that news. As early as 16 August 1819, the *Times* was testing its newly minted liberal credentials in its coverage of Peterloo which incidentally was one of the first events to be covered live by newspaper reporters in any great number. The *Times* subsequently established an early reputation for political pragmatism as a key component of this brand of respectable journalism as identified by Hazlitt:

> The *Times* fights no uphill battle, advocates no great principle, holds out a helping hand to no oppressed or obscure individual; it is 'ever strong upon the stronger side;' its style is magniloquent, its spirit is not magnanimous . . . Stuffed with official documents, with matter-of-fact details, it might be imagined to be composed, as well as printed, with a steam-engine . . . It sells more, and contains more, than any other paper, and when you have said this you have said all. (*Edinburgh Review*, May 1823: 362–364)

The combination of John Walter II's business enterprise and Barnes editorial skills established the newspaper's reputation. Barnes recruited and remunerated the best writers including Edward Sterling, the leader writer who penned the celebrated article which gained the nickname 'The Thunderer' for the paper. Harrison has pointed out that it had been a staunch supporter of the oligarchy but moved strategically from 1830 in step with the liberal sentiments of its readers (Harrison, 1974: 99), to support the Reform Bill in language which has resonated down the years. On 29 January 1831 Stirling wrote, in support of voting reform proposals for the propertied middle classes:

> unless the people – the people everywhere – come forward and petition, ay thunder for reform, it is they who abandon an honest Minister – it is *not* the Minister who betrays the people.

Francis Williams has commented of the dominance and influence of the *Times* that it was by the mid-century:

> a towering Everest of a newspaper with sales ten times those of any other daily, combining leadership in circulation, in news services especially of the most confidential and exclusive kind – in advertising revenue, commercial profit and political influence to an extent no other newspaper anywhere in the world has ever done before or since. (1957: 100)

To complement this commercial dominance, the *Times* took on the mantle as a spokespiece for assertive journalism. It was established as the 'Jove of the press' (Andrews, 1998, Vol. 2: 209) when in 1852 it was able to clarify, on its own terms, the respective roles and responsibilities of the press and statesmen. In response to Lord Derby in the *Times* on 6 and 7 February 1852, it outlined its own vision of a fully independent Fourth Estate:

> The press lives by disclosures; whatever passes into its keeping becomes a part of the knowledge and history of our times; it is daily and for ever appealing to the enlightened force of public opinion – anticipating, if possible, the march of events – standing upon the breach between the present and the future, and extending its survey to the horizon of the world. The statesman's duty is precisely the reverse. He cautiously guards from the public eye the information by which his actions and opinions are regulated; he reserves his judgement on passing events till the latest moment, and then he records it in obscure or conventional language; he strictly confines himself, if he be wise, to the practical interests of his own country, or to those bearing immediately upon it; he hazards no rash surmises as to the future; and he concentrates in his own transactions all that power which the press seeks to diffuse over the world. The duty of the one is to speak; of the other to be silent.

Its role in domestic politics was soon to be enhanced by a growing reputation for an ability to convey the latest and best information from abroad, deploying its networks of reporters and agents to bring news back from the war in the Crimea from 1854 quicker than government communications could manage. William Howard Russell had first come to prominence reporting the Irish potato famine in 1845 and 1846 and was to bring regular, colourful, eyewitness accounts of foreign wars to readers' breakfast tables for the first time and more importantly a critical eye able to shift public opinion on the state of the armed forces and the conduct of their leaders in war. He covered the Crimean and subsequently the American Civil War, the Austro-Prussian War 1866 and the Franco-Prussian war 1870–1871. Delane was able to exploit this coverage to lend increased authority to his leading articles as in this example:

> The noblest army ever sent from these shores has been sacrificed to the grossest mismanagement. Incompetency, lethargy, aristocratic hauteur, official indifference, favour, routine, perverseness, and stupidity reign, revel and riot in the camp before Sebastopol, in the harbour of Balaklava, in the hospital of Scutari, and how much nearer home we do not venture to say. (The *Times*, 23 December 1854)

Among other things, it was the achievements of the *Times* during the Crimean War which enabled it to emerge as the champion of enlightened patriotic opinion and this was endorsed by much critical discussion among the influential quarterlies of the era:

> Ministers, even by their own admission, learned the state of affairs in the Crimea sooner, more fully, and more faithfully, through the

columns of the daily journals than from their own dispatches. (Reeve, 1855: 483)

The Crimean War was significant for the development of the newspaper in the way it demonstrated a material political power. The *Times* contributed directly to the fall of a government, the creation of the post of Secretary of State for War, and the intervention of Florence Nightingale which was to alter public perceptions of the rights of wounded combatants to medical support. Russell established that the occupation of a reporter was to go and find out what is happening, which is the basic premise of investigative journalism (De Burgh, 2000: 34). Increasingly, its news was characteristic of a time of great imperial confidence, reflecting that '. . . the standpoint of the reader was assumed to be that of someone with a serious concern for the affairs of a world power' (Brown, 1985: 111). Yet despite its undoubted authority in foreign correspondence, the prestige of the *Times* was based on a completeness of parliamentary reporting which would not survive as a model of newspaper best practice for too long. In its desire to reinforce its reputation as the provider of the best and most complete accounts of political affairs, it would produce page after page of unbroken, verbatim speeches from Parliament. This would soon provide the spur for other newspapers to develop a differentiation between their content and their style through the process of editing but for the moment, as the *Times* reigned supreme, newspapers had not yet evolved a style distinct from their subject matter:

> The news had not yet developed the textual apparatus of interviewing, summarizing, quoting and editing that would allow it to be able to claim to represent reality . . . Even when papers' reporters gathered information themselves, the style was shaped by the style of the topic of the text. The *Times'* law reports, for example, used a vocabulary and syntax strongly reminiscent of the courts. (Matheson, 2000: 562–563)

Commercializing popular politics: *Reynolds's Weekly Newspaper*

Although sometimes related as the most important development in nineteenth-century journalism, the *Times* was far from the whole story. On 5 February 1836, the last conviction of an unstamped paper is thought to have been of a police weekly when John Cleave was fined 500 pounds in the Court of the Exchequer for publishing five numbers of a newspaper called the *Weekly Police Gazette* (Andrews (1998), Vol. 2: 227), but from now on the official publication of crime news and other forms of sensational story began to play a more prominent role in nearly all newspapers.

The first successful mass newspapers in England were the Sunday newspapers. These Sunday newspapers were *Lloyd's Illustrated London Newspaper* (1842), the *News of the World* (1843) and *Reynolds's Weekly Newspaper* (1850). They all managed a skilful combination of radical rhetoric and elements of popular cultural continuity: 'all radical, or at least Liberal, all catering for sensation, all containing stories and illustrations' (Lee, 1976: 71). Their most spectacular combination of the sensational, the radical and the nationalistic came in their coverage of the Crimean war. They were popular in reach because of their ability to articulate aspects of everyday life and to express it in a language identifiable as belonging to its audience. The emergence of the popular Sundays in Britain is much closer chronologically and generically with the emergence of the Penny Press in the United States. It is as if, loosed from the restrictions of the taxes on knowledge and bound into an expanding capital market, the popular newspaper could only have moved in one direction. The same seems to be true of the development of the popular press at about this time in France (Palmer, 1983).

The commercial success of these newspapers may have incorporated the views of the general public, but it was firmly anchored in the established tradition and style of the broadside, almanac and ballad form which had previously acted before all else as profit makers for the printers and publishers. These newspapers learnt how to combine these elements in a manner which made them accessible to a readership eager to learn about the world and to be entertained, but in ways which did not demand too much direct reflection on political concerns despite the fact that *Reynolds*, for example, was at first committed to support the six points of the People's Charter. Vincent argues that the popular press played a large part in developing a commercial genre which: 'in translating the discrimination of news into a completely new category of popular leisure coincided with the virtual disappearance of working-class politics' (Vincent, 1993: 252). Perhaps the disappearance of working-class political newspapers was more of an incorporation of working-class politics into a style which favoured the emerging bourgeois consensus, not in the hurly burly of political debate but rather in a radically new form of consumer-spectator society.

Lloyd's, *Reynolds's* and the *News of the World* made profits by successfully and regularly addressing the lower classes, by playing to the passions of a popular audience with a radical tone but one divorced from either calls to organize politically or to engage in any broader political analysis. This constituted a commercialization of the radical voice. Sunday newspapers in particular were drawn more to the popular genre of melodrama as a means to maximize readerships with all of this genre's ideological and social implications. It drew upon the still popular genre of 'last dying speeches' and related narratives of transgression and punishment. Melodrama represents the world as a stark set of contrasts between good and evil (Brooks, 1984) and without much in the way of analysis as to the causes of antisocial or criminal behaviour beyond blame attached to individuals. However, Knelman (1992) argues that melodrama was a broader discourse within mid-Victorian prose than simply fodder for the Sunday newspapers and claims that the mid-Victorian press generally used the techniques of melodramatic fiction in presenting the darker sides of social life including rudimentary psychological analyses, a fascination with shocking detail and calls for justice and retribution even before the courts' pronouncements, and just as the Victorian novelists presented a moral code so too did the journalists present the material of real life to reinforce prevailing standards of behaviour (Knelman, 1992: 35).

At the start, *Reynolds's Weekly Newspaper* was a miscellany of political commentary, news with a special appeal to the interests of the working class plus sensational stories of bizarre events, crimes and gossip as well as more traditional newspaper fare such as court reports, notices to correspondents and advertisements. The publisher's ideas were prominently displayed, often signed by him on the front page.

In *Reynolds's Weekly* for 7 July 1850 'The proletarian's career from the cradle to the grave', ends:

> How immense are the abuses which render our social system abhorrent to the humane man and terrible to the thoughtful one! – how undeserved are the honours, the luxuries, and the blessings which the favoured few enjoy – are how tremendous are the woes, the wrongs, and the cruelties, which the millions endure . . . One wholesale annihilation of the abuse, on the one hand, and one unlimited acknowledgement of rights on the other, can alone save this country from chaos – from anarchy – from ruin. The People's Charter, as the means towards the reconstruction of the social system, is the only panacea, the only remedy.

Berridge notes that the language of political discourse in *Reynolds's Weekly* is similar to that in the theatre and popular fiction which was drawn in large part from Reynolds's own experience of writing novels (Berridge, 1978: 253–254). However, there was a political aspect to the dominance of the melodramatic in the Sunday papers which subtly discouraged a genuine political engagement on behalf of its readers:

> The political discourse in *Reynolds's Weekly* divides and totalises the political 'facts' into implacable evil and unbeatable good.

> But while it validates the struggle between these two forces, it denies the inevitability of any final social disruption. (Humpherys, 1990: 45)

By the late Victorian heyday of these popular Sunday newspapers, any initial radicalism had been subsumed into a popular representation of the activities of the crowd, as in the example below, with a political distance between the report and the possible motivations of the demonstrators. It is a long way from even the 'old corruption' rhetoric of the early-century publicists who overtly sided with the concerns of the crowd and who wrote from a perspective partisan to their viewpoint. The tiered headlines introducing this extract showed that the initial focus is on the effects not the causes of the demonstration.

> SERIOUS RIOTING IN LONDON
> SCENE IN TRAFALGAR SQUARE
> WEST END SHOPS WRECKED
> EXTRAORDINARY PANIC

> On Monday, in the interest of the unemployed of London, a demonstration of a very mixed character and ended in disorder, was held in Trafalgar-square. The original meeting was called by the labourers' league, who thought to stimulate the authorities in proceeding with works of relief. The occasion was seized some Fair Trade leaguers of the east-end to pose before the public as the exponents of working class opinion, and also by the body called the 'Revolutionary Social Democratic Federation,' who had given out that they would seize the platforms of the other demonstrators . . . For a time the roughs quite defied the police, and a red flag was waved above them. Some of the mob pelted the police with flour . . . (14 February 1886)

Long accounts, including all possible details of events and appearance drawing upon the melodramatic narrative conventions of the Victorian novel are mapped onto the detail and chronology of court reporting:

> Mr Hicks opened an inquiry at the workhouse, Wallis's-yard, Buckingham-palace-road, on Thursday, touching the death of Edwin Thomas Bartlett, aged 40, partner in a firm of grocers and provision dealers, carrying on business at Station-road Herne-hill, and other places, and who died at 85, Claverton-street Pimlico, on New Year's day, under peculiar circumstances.
>   Edwin Bartlett, deceased's father, stated that his son was married 12 years ago, his wife being under age at the time. For two years she did not live with the deceased, but completed her education abroad. She then lived with him at Herne-hill, Merton Abbey, and Dover. In October last they went to 85, Claverton-street, where they occupied furnished rooms. Deceased's health, had been remarkably

good until shortly before Christmas, when he became ill. Witnesses saw him two or three times, and could not account for his illness. On a subsequent occasion Mrs Bartlett refused to allow him to see his son, stating that he was too ill to receive visitors. On December 28 he received a letter from her and went to the house, and had a long interview with his son, who although queer in his manner, appeared very confident of speedy recovery. He told witness that in the doctor's opinion his illness had arisen from mercurial poisoning, but he could not understand how he could have taken such a poison, as he never used mercury in his business. Something was also said about lead poisoning, the deceased remarking that he had opened many tea chests, and might have been poisoned in that way. The conversation took place in the presence of Mrs Bartlett. On Jan. 1 witness was telegraphed for, and found his son dead. He insisted on a post mortem examination by independent medical men . . . (10 January 1886)

An excellent example of the sort of narrative description of character comes in the presentation of Mrs Bartlett at her trial during the notorious 'Pimlico Mystery'.

Mrs. Bartlett's eyes were drooping, and she stood motionless with arms straight down the sides – a small figure, without hat or bonnet, shawl or mantle, but wearing a well-fitting black silk dress, relieved by something white at the neck, and she was conspicuous by the great shock of short black hair which surmounted a somewhat broad and sallow face. (18 April 1886)

Charles Dickens: Social narratives between fiction and non-fiction

Dickens's influence on the development of nineteenth-century newspaper language was of enormous significance (Tulloch, 2007) because of his connections to the most prominent fictional authors of the day and his impact as editor and journalist on a generation of journalists who succeeded him such as Yates, Jerrold, Sala, his 'young men' (Edwards, 1997). He provides the fullest demonstration of the mutual influence of fiction and non-fiction in the mid-Victorian age in his urban reportage and his ability to recreate the patterns of popular speech (Tulloch, 2007: 66). As befits an author who straddled these generic fields he uses a wealth of literary, including biblical allusion, drawn from the store of general education available at the time. His journalism is a veritable treasure chest of Victorian popular culture and demonstrates the more efficient and profitable representation of social knowledge which popular journalism took upon itself in the nineteenth century as a 'specialised role within the social observance of reality' (Smith, 1978: 165). Dickens worked on the *Morning Chronicle* from 1834 but it was his contributions to the *Examiner* from 1837–1843 and then from 1848–1849, that Brice and Fielding claim helped form his interest in society, and shifts his style from reporter to journalist (Brice and Fielding, 1981: 1). His writing began to encompass social commentary, satire and dialogue as it moved from lively reportage to 'brilliantly inventive and entertaining journalism' (Slater, 1997: xx).

Interspersed with a running commentary on the play in progress at a popular theatre, Dickens uses his fictional character Mr Whelks to consider the tastes and entertainments of the lower classes of the metropolis in brilliant pastiche:

> The Amusements of the People
>
> As one half of the world is said not to know how the other half lives, so it may be affirmed that the upper half of the world neither knows nor greatly cares how the lower half amuses itself. Believing that it does not care because it does not know, we purpose occasionally recording a few facts on the subject.
>
> The general character of the lower class of dramatic amusements is a very significant sign of a people, and a very good test of their intellectual condition. We design to make our readers acquainted in the first place with a few of our experiences under this head in the metropolis . . .
>
> Joe Whelks of the New Cut, Lambeth, is not much of a reader, has no great store of books, no very commodious room to read in, no very decided inclination to read, and no power at all of presenting vividly before his mind's eye what he reads about. But put Joe in the gallery of the Victoria Theatre; show him doors and windows in the scene that will open and shut, and that people can get in and out of; tell him a story with these aids, and by the help of live men and women dressed up, confiding to him their innermost secrets, in voices audible half a mile off; and Joe will unravel a story through all its entanglements, and sit there as long after midnight as you have anything left to show him . . .
>
> The company in the pit were not very clean or sweet-savoured, but there were some good-humoured mechanics among them, with their wives. These were generally accompanied by 'the baby' insomuch that the pit was a perfect nursery. No effect made on the stage was so curious, as the looking down on the quiet faces of these babies fast asleep, after looking up at the staring sea of heads in the gallery. There were a good many cold fried soles in the pit, besides; and a variety of flat stone bottles, of all portable sizes . . .
> (*Household Words*, 30 March 1850)

The *Daily Telegraph*: Exploring the potential of liberalization

We have already noted the accuracy of Chalaby's (1998) claims that the modern discourse of journalism takes shape at the specific point when market mechanisms begin to dominate the ownership, strategies and competitive practices of public writing after 1855. The period also saw the nature of news itself become increasingly refined. The establishment in 1851 of Reuter's News Agency began to ensure a regular and more homogenous supply of routine news. This had the result of easing the chief problem of previous newspapers – the irregular flow of news for a daily press. News had always been a commodity but it was now able to become a more streamlined and capitalized commodity. It was no longer simply an addition to a publisher's portfolio but a prized product in its own right and an invaluable conduit to the advertisers' revenue.

In 1853, advertising duty was abolished which added to the commercial revenues upon which the newspapers and magazines were increasingly dependent. In 1855, stamp duty was abolished; to take immediate advantage, the *Daily Telegraph* was founded as the *Daily Telegraph and Courier* on 29 June 1955 and heralded its arrival, not without a certain prescience, as, '. . . the new era of journalism . . .' The *Daily Telegraph* was the most successful daily experiment on the lifting of taxes. It looked the same as its competitors but was the first London morning paper to sell for a penny. It quickly established an identity which distinguished it from the deliberate elitism of the *Times*: 'The *Times*, the paper for the City merchant, and the *Daily Telegraph*, the paper for the clerk and shopkeeper' (Brown, 1985: 246). It still gave many columns over to leading articles and contained serious and authoritative letters to the editor but it was the ability of Edward Levy to introduce elements of the human interest of American popular journalism to the paper which broadened its appeal and success. As a popularizer, Levy was the forerunner of Stead and Northcliffe:

> 'What we want is a human note' was the instruction of J.M. Levy to his young entrants . . . [his] intention was to produce something different from other newspapers in which politics were presumed to be the only interest of the reader. (Burnham: 76–77)

It produced one of the most important new developments in Victorian journalism in its public campaigning around the concerns of its readers. A celebrated example of this is its coverage of one of the great moral dilemmas of the Victorian age, the hitherto taboo subject of the recourse of respectable middle-class men to prostitution as they delayed marriage until they were financially secure to provide for a wife. Although this provoked understandable accusations of sensationalism and prurience, it did establish a new form of relationship with its readers beyond these factors. It built on the letters of readers, already an established tradition, but with the novel twist that they enabled the paper to emphasize its contact with this readership and its voice, in creating a concerted and large-scale debate. As a result of this strategy, it has been credited with the creation of a more participatory journalism, 'moving authority from leaders to Readers . . .' (Robson, 1995: 260). The language of the launch of the campaign indicates something of the rhetorical inclusion of the reader within the paper's project: '. . . the army of public pity and indignation . . . a new Crusade . . . a moral Armada of hope and effort . . . a vast body of public opinion . . .' (Robson, 1995: 17).

From its first edition, it signalled an editorial coup in providing abbreviated accounts of the proceedings of Parliament, to provide for an audience with less leisure and interest in the verbatim accounts of the *Times* and in deference to a belief that a wider readership wanted a broader digest of the contemporary world:

> Our readers will perceive that, in place of reporting the proceedings of Parliament in full, we give a copious summary, in the belief that the great majority of readers of the Daily Press will prefer the pith and marrow of the Debates to the lengthened reports presented every morning in the columns of our contemporaries. (20 June 1855)

In order to sustain this newly mined popularity, it devoted a whole page to reports of a riot, pickpocketing, bankruptcy, child maintenance and domestic violence. There was, for instance, a graphic account of the witness taking the stand in a child maintenance case:

> Mr Hutchinson having called Mrs. Thatcher, an elegant and lady-like personage, as soon as the chief usher administered the oath, she instantly fell down in the witness-box, striking her face upon the floor with a sickening rebound, and for some time it was considered that the fall and the excitement would end fatally. (20 June 1855)

The *Daily Telegraph* was, within a few years, selling more than all other London dailies combined, including the *Times*. It included a growing number of writers, including George Augustus Sala from 1858, who wrote in a livelier fashion than had been the custom in the serious daily papers and reached out to a broader section of the middle classes. The self-consciously decorative and effusive language which came to be known as Telegraphese would have drawn its cultural capital from the

Victorian appreciation of rich writing and descriptive writing in general, from the periods of master stylists such as Carlyle or Macauley or Gibbon (Matheson, 2000: 561). Sala was hugely versatile moving from social to literary commentary and then to a self-defined role as Special Commissioner in Russia, and in America during the Civil War as well as in wars in Europe. He was for many years the best known of the *Daily Telegraph's* 'Young Lions,' claiming innovative interview subjects for the newspaper in Napoleon III in 1865 and Garibaldi in 1866. He worked well within the more popular tone and broader social scope of the *Daily Telegraph* and has been claimed to be a pioneer for later developments in the language of newspaper of the late nineteenth century:

> He wrote light leaders and reported exuberantly on overseas and domestic events for the paper. His fluid 'pen-pictures' influenced a generation of popular writers, and, perhaps more than any other journalist, he helped to create a style of 'bright,' human interest writing that was to become so integral a part of the New Journalism . . . (Wiener, 1996: 63)

By the 1870s, the use of numerous headlines to lead an important news story was one of the more noticeable innovations in terms of its layout. The invention by the paper of the box number for advertisements is a clear indication of its acumen in exploiting the new economic opportunities for daily newspapers. The combination of its commercial and linguistic flair ensured that it had a sale of 200,000 by the 1880s. There was, however, resistance to its new brand of journalism. The *Pall Mall Gazette* made frequent disparaging remarks about *Daily Telegraph* referring to it on 9 January 1868 as a 'quack journal' because of its association with cheap doctors and patent medicine cures; whereas in the same year, the *Saturday Review's* two articles on 'Newspaper Sewage' on 5 December and 12 December 1868 were a clear indictment of the moral tone of the *Daily Telegraph* and its nearest competitors, the *Standard* and the *Morning Star*.

The gradual erosion of anonymity

The flamboyant and easily identifiable writing of Sala and the subsequent rise of celebrated and named journalists on particular papers led inexorably to the decline of absolute anonymity which had been until the mid-Victorian period one of the anchors of journalistic integrity. Anonymity was directly linked to the belief of newspaper owners and editors that argument could be won and opinion moulded without recourse to the personal reputation of the writer. It was very much part of the work which newspaper editors had begun to perfect from the late eighteenth century; to shape the convictions of the newspaper, organically, towards a much more homogenized approach which could enhance the positioning of a particular newspaper within a specific niche of the market where readers would come to expect a certain approach or framing to the newspaper's coverage. The gradual demise of anonymity was a significant element in the growth of the related trends of personalization and popularization in the newspaper which would continue to drive developments in their language and their overall approach to readerships throughout the late nineteenth and twentieth centuries.

Conclusion

The newspaper of the nineteenth century was a complex formation which moved to incorporate the impacts of the Reform Acts of 1832, 1867, 1884 with their implications for the relationship between politics and a widening, enfranchised public. This complexity was added to by rapidly evolving technological, economic and demographic changes which all share intersecting chronologies with that of the newspaper. The confluence of news agencies and the development of the telegraph brought a much more reliable and economical flow of information and dictated the emphasis on news which began to dominate the daily press. Reuter set up an office in London in 1851 to provide commercial intelligence and in 1858 extended this to foreign digests of news to London papers. Private news transmission by telegraph began in 1866 together with further developments in communications, especially the telephone, allowed the practice of 'double-checking' of sources to become established within journalism and is considered to be one of its defining modern characteristics (Smith, 1978: 155). As the supply of news increased because of better transport and technologies of communication, the newspaper needed to be better managed. Newspapers were able to claim authority on their own terms as they now went beyond the provision of complete or shortened verbatim accounts of public proceedings. There was an increasing impact of developments in the popular press on the elite press as the years went by although always with a dignified time lag. The key date was, however, 1855 after which all newspapers were in open competition for readers and for advertisers. The consequences of these changes were profound, leading to a demarcation between roles and between genres in newspaper production and content; an increasingly class-based polarization between elite and popular newspapers.

5 A message from America: A commercial vernacular

Introduction

The American influence on the shaping of the language of the English newspaper is nowhere more evident than in the nineteenth century as the newspaper moved from addressing a politically motivated readership to a more general mass public. Schudson asserts the explicitly American influence on the shaping of journalism in general, as practice and discourse:

> Journalism is not something that floated platonically above the world and that each country copied down, shaping it to its own natural grammar. It is something that – as we know it today – Americans had a major hand in inventing. (Schudson, 2008: 187)

The American penny dailies of the 1830s were the first newspapers to attempt to write consistently and commercially for a broad social stratum of ordinary people in a voice which attempted to capture something of the vitality of everyday speech. It would be no exaggeration to claim that they provided a primer in a new vernacular for increasing numbers of immigrant readers. Furthermore, the language of these newspapers which began to articulate a wider social range of language helped broaden the definition of news by embracing a more complete spectrum of the lived experience of daily life in the expanding American cities. They soon systematized this into a repertoire of stories and strategies, a coverage of crime and deployment of interviews, which could lay claim to have encapsulated a commercialized version of the interests of the ordinary people. Later in the century, these strategies were developed in an intensifying commercial struggle between the New York newspaper owners, Pulitzer and Hearst. The success of these new forms of popular journalism became a factor in the development of newspapers in Britain as they too sought to appeal to wider audiences after 1855. However, the more entrenched class distinctions in British society meant that each newspaper carved out a particular socio-political niche for itself, often based more on specific articulations of social class. At first, it had been the Sunday newspapers which provided a commercially successful appeal to the working people in Britain while various London-based daily newspapers tried, with varying degrees of success, to attract readers from a widening middle class. By the end of the century, under the influence of the American popular press, the British version of the New Journalism would begin to reshape the style and content of much of the national press with its emphasis on sensationalism, typographical changes and the adoption of a familiar tone with its readers. The most significant developments in popular journalism at this time, both in the United States and Britain, were to have a major impact on the structure of newspapers' language for the next hundred years as the story began to usurp the report as the main format of the newspapers (Matheson, 2000) with all the implications that this has for the prioritizing and framing of social narratives (Entmann, 1993).

The democratic tradition

The strong democratic tradition within American political culture which emerged as a key factor in fashioning emancipation from the British Empire found full expression in periodical and pamphlet publication. Rhetorically at least, this tradition could be called upon with consistency and authority when the American newspaper began its engagement with wider-based popular audiences from the early nineteenth century. One of the best examples of the journalist as a political propagandist on behalf of the people in the years prior to the American War of Independence was Samuel Adams who from a radical perspective contributed to the *Boston Gazette and Country Journal* as well as acting as editor for the *Independent Advertiser*. Emery and Emery have highlighted the main rhetorical features he required to make such public writing persuasive and therefore successful:

> He understood that to win the inevitable conflict, he and his cohorts must achieve five main objectives. They must justify the course they advocated. They must advertise the advantages of victory. They must arouse the masses – the real shock troops – by instilling hatred of enemies. They must neutralize and logical and reasonable arguments proposed by the opposition. And finally, they must phrase all the issues in black and white, so that the purposes might be clear even to the common laborer. Adams was able to do all this, and his principal tool was the colonial newspaper. (Emery and Emery, 1992: 46–47)

Thomas Paine, whose influence on English radicalism has already been explored, also contributed to the creation of a democratic radical rhetoric in American journalism. He wrote for the *Pennsylvania Magazine* for long enough to establish a reputation as a fine polemicist on issues such as slavery, universal suffrage and education. In 1776, *Common Sense* is credited with bringing the less radical Patriots into the revolutionary movement. It had an enormous and instant success, selling 120,000 copies in 3 months (Emery and Emery, 1992: 53). We must bear this tradition of popular rhetoric in mind, addressed to the ordinary citizens of an emergent democracy, if we are to understand the reasons for the enormous success of the penny papers of the 1830s. However, what transformed this democratic rhetoric into cheap popular newspapers was less a popular demand for a direct political address and more the impact of mechanization during the Industrial Revolution which ensured that lower production and distribution costs could effect an extension of the traditionally narrow readerships which the middle class American press had helped to maintain (Mott, 1962: 215). There were two complementary aspects to the newspaper revolution. One was the improved efficiencies in technology and news-gathering strategies which allowed news to be first collected and then distributed more profitably than ever. Technological advances in printing enabled a cheaper paper to be sold not for 6 cents but for a single cent, but this demanded a larger readership to cover costs more immediately than the older system of longer-term subscriptions would allow. The cheaper papers, therefore, broke with the tradition of selling on subscription, which implied a long-standing financial commitment to a particular newspaper, and shifted to being sold on the street on a daily basis which made for a more ephemeral contest for the attention of the passer-by. The second change, emerging from the appeal to a new clientele, was an attempt to rediscover something of the rhetorical appeal to the people which had been used so successfully by the radical journalists of the previous century. This time the language of the ordinary people was inflected to commercial rather than political ends. Nerone traces the popular expansion of the American press in the nineteenth century explicitly to the ideas and aspirations for democratic participation in society triggered by the American Revolution:

> The expansion of the press in the United States was a result of ideas and expectations popularized in the American Revolution. This change, beginning in the eighteenth century, was deeply affected by two grand developments in the nineteenth century: the rise of popular partisan politics and the appearance of a market economy. (Nerone, 1987: 377)

It is generally considered (Douglas, 1999: 1–9) that it was during the Jackson presidency that the civic self-confidence and egalitarianism of the Revolution came to flourish in a popular press which drew upon older traditions of the vulgar populism of American broadsheets and

97

ballads (Nordin, 1979) to establish a profitable representation of the everyday interests of the ordinary American people. The confidence of this era allowed newspapers to sell a sense of political and social involvement back to the people as readers and in a language which sought to recapture something of the excitement of everyday life's trials, scandals and tragedies. In turn, this new colloquialism could claim to have established the bond between reader and paper which would ensure a continuing commercial success.

To underline its democratizing address to the common reader, the first of the successful penny dailies, the *New York Sun* was launched on 3 September 1833 by Benjamin H. Day with its motto: 'It Shines For ALL'. Schiller has placed this in the foreground of a radical realignment of newspapers' engagement with the wider public:

> The motto, profoundly captured the democratic promise of the penny press: the extension of public access to information and met-amorphosis of the character of public information itself . . . By giving all citizens an equal access to knowledge and direct personal knowledge of impartially presented news, the penny press could boast of its thorough revision of the language of the public sphere. (Schiller, 1981: 48)

The *New York Sun* provided fresh, topical news and presented it in a concise manner, emphasizing the local with human interest and often sensational events at its core. Court reporting, including the verbatim vernacular of the proceedings themselves fitted this pattern and was enormously popular. These reports were often the source of a mockery which highlighted the ambivalence of popular newspapers to parts of their target audience. The vernacular could in itself be a source of humour for the newspaper with which to entertain a readership which fancied itself a cut above the pathetic participants of daily court activity. Stevens (1991: 24) has exemplified the mocking mimicry of these court reports, for example, 'Honrable Honor', 'Jontlemen of the jury' to 'plade' her own cause. The humorous recounting of police-court news had been developed in *Cleaves Weekly Police Gazette* in London which shows that the flow between the United States and Britain was not entirely one-way traffic. It consisted of a set of influences between jour-nalism traditions very much framed within the economics and political possibilities of specific social environments. This meant that while the United States got broad-based penny daily newspapers, Britain was developing a range of popular Sunday newspapers directed specifi-cally at the working classes within a commercialized idiom. If the new penny newspapers took the public sphere to the streets, then its court reporting brought the streets back to the public as entertainment and information. In addition to its editorial features, the inclusion of small classified advertisements in the *Sun* was an important innovation in that it reinforced the attractiveness of this new penny newspaper to a hitherto neglected audience. They were sold by space rates for cash (instead of on an annual basis, which was the practice of the other papers), especially the 'Help Wanted' notices (Crouthamel, 1989: 20) making it popular with the unemployed.

Gordon Bennett's *New York Herald*

The success of the *Sun* encouraged competitors to vie for the affections and curiosity of a new newspaper-reading public. The most significant in terms of its contribution to the evolving language of the newspaper was James Gordon Bennett's *New York Herald*. Even as a court-reporter at the *Courier and Enquirer,* he had referred to the newspaper as a medium of popular enlightenment, in terms reminiscent of the Revolutionary press, identifying what he thought was the democratic role of the newspaper in expressing the views of the people on contemporary events: 'The press is the *living jury* of the nation' (Crouthamel, 1989: 13).

As well as being an opportunist with a well-developed sense of historical timing, he could also lay claim to having a fairly consistent democratic tone to his politics. This had, once again, been clear from his early days in journalism at the *Courier and Enquirer*:

> An editor must always be with the people – think with them – feel with them – and he need fear nothing, he will always be right – always be strong – always popular – always free. (12 November 1931 in Mott, 1962: 232)

This sort of populism might have been simple commercial common sense but it is certainly an approach he perfected as his *New York Herald* rose to a dominant position on account of its wide circulation (77,000 in 1860 made it the world's largest sale). It provided a lively, concise account of the day of the city with crime, gossip, sport and business news. It also took a keen interest in using the interview to develop crime reporting.

Its use during the Robinson-Jewett murder case in 1836 was signifi-cant not just in terms of the technique itself but in the way that Bennett used the structure of the interview to frame the language in terms of the social and political commentary of the paper, as a spokespiece for the values of ordinary people against the privileged classes and, most importantly, in creating a textual collusion between the vitality of this reporting of direct speech and the speech patterns of the readers. The case involved the murder of a prostitute, Jewett, in New York and provided an ideal opportunity to package many of the traditional features of popular melodrama into the format of the penny paper with all the additional advantages that running the story on a daily basis could bring, constantly embroidering it with the latest sensational details for a large contemporary audience. The suspicion fell on a young and wealthy socialite, Robinson, and in taking the side of the murdered prostitute, Bennett was able to appeal to the curiosity of his readers, their sense of sympathy with a poor victim and rail against the hypocrisies of the wealthy. He provided editorial commentary which reflected directly on the inequity of the treatment of the poor by the criminal justice system and combined these factors to justify his intrusive, personality-based news coverage as a campaign for social improvement.

On April 11, the front page was dominated by the news and the lead editorial in the *Herald* was headed: 'Most Atrocious Murder'.

On his third visit to the house, he conducted his famous interview with the proprietor, Mrs Townsend:

> Did you hear no other noise previous to the knocking of the young man to let you in?
>
> I think I heard a noise and said who's there, but received no answer.
>
> How did you know that the person you let in was Frank (the alias Robinson used at the house)?
>
> He gave his name.
>
> Did you see his face?
>
> No – his cloak was held up over his face. I saw nothing but his eyes as he passed me – he had on a hat and a coat. (17 April 1836)

He justified his coverage in the face of a hostile reception from the respectable press by emphasizing its role as a social commentary with the potential to shake a complacent nation:

> Instead of relating the recent awful tragedy of Ellen Jewett as a dull police report, we made it the starting point to open up a full view upon the morals of society – the hinge of a course of mental action calculated to benefit the age – the opening scene of a great domestic drama that will, if properly conducted, bring about a reformation – a revolution – a total revolution in the present diseased state of society and morals. (Crouthamel, 1989: 30)

As a populist, there was also a darker side to Bennett's political convictions. He shared many of the nationalistic sentiments of the readers he so astutely courted and in trying to match these tastes, he was a regular editorial contributor to debates about America's mission in the world, known to contemporaries as 'Manifest Destiny'. His patriotic convictions often stepped over into chauvinism and xenophobia as in the following example:

> The Anglo-Saxon race is intended by an overruling Providence to carry the principles of liberty, the refinements of civilisation, and the advantages of the mechanical era through every land, even those now barbarous. The prostrate savage and the benighted heathen, shall yet be imbued with Anglo-Saxon intelligence and culture, and be blessed with the institutions, both civil and religious, which are now our inheritance. Mexico, too, must submit to the o'erpowering influence of the Anglo-Saxon. (Crouthamel, 1989: 57)

Bennett's *Herald* became the first newspaper to develop the society reporting which was to become the forerunner of celebrity-based news. Bennett's approach was novel in the way it placed an old genre within a new aspirant capitalist democracy. The genre itself was as old as printed communication – gossip about social superiors – but in the market meritocracy of mid-century America it offered a more flattened form of social representation than the public sphere of the middle-class periodicals.

The general achievements of the penny dailies

Beyond New York, the *Philadelphia Public Ledger*, and the *Baltimore Sun* as well the *Daily Times* in Boston all contributed to the generation of a new class of newspaper readers. An important aspect for their development was the Mexican War (1846–1848). War might traditionally increase newspaper sales but it might also be observed that it is one of the prime catalysts in shifts in newspaper language. This was never truer than during this period when the new printing technologies and populist appeal of the Penny Press merged in the coverage of the Mexican War. There were frequent etched illustrations of battle scenes and strategic battle plans. Headlines in multiple decks over big stories became commonplace. By the late 1840s there was a tendency to extend them vertically for big stories, spacing them out and adding more decks until they might occupy nearly half a column (Mott, 1962: 292) Larger headlines led to the omission of verbs and a language which matched the populism and patriotic assertiveness which Bennett had found was such a productive ingredient in his journalism.

The rise of the Penny Press and the perception, at least, of the political potency of the common people in the Jacksonian era were closely related. Schudson supports this view while adding that the Penny Press emerged in response to the needs of what he calls a 'democratic market society', which he identifies as having three main characteristics: the consolidation of a mass democracy, an ideology of the marketplace and an increasingly urban society. The new papers, he claims:

> were spokesmen for egalitarian ideals in politics, economic life and social life through their organization of sales, their solicitation of advertising, their emphasis on news, their catering to large audiences and their decreasing concern with the editorial . . . (Schudson, 1978: 60)

Economics always has an important cultural aspect and it was the cultural component of the mid-century popular American newspapers which connected the folk traditions of popular readerships with the political expectations of the Revolutionary tradition within an early market economy. Thus the earliest popular penny papers were enacting a form of inclusive hegemony, binding their readers into the project of American market-democratic modernity by speaking their language.

Joseph Pulitzer's New Journalism

The *New York World* was revived by Joseph Pulizer in 1883 and from the day he took over he embraced and extended the techniques introduced by the Penny Press (Stevens, 1991: 99). In his first edition he stressed that his paper was:

> . . . not only large but truly democratic – dedicated to the cause of the people rather than to that of the purse potentates – devoted more to the New World than the Old World – that will expose all fraud and sham, fight all public evils and abuses – that will battle for the people with earnest sincerity. (Mott, 1962: 434)

He developed the style of his paper to better appeal to the poorer classes, those who were unaccustomed to reading a daily newspaper, the migrants to the burgeoning cities and the immigrants to the new nation. All these helped to establish the economic base for a newer, truly mass journalism and simultaneously they were all becoming drawn into the textual constructing of a new style of imagined community (Anderson, 1986). The aspects of this New Journalism which made it such an effective representation of the culture of its popular audience comprised four complementary strategies: a rhetoric which mimicked the voice and supposed opinions of the working people; a broad match between the news values of the newspaper and the everyday interests of this same audience; a high reliance on entertainment and sensation; an appeal to a specifically national audience which reinforced chauvinist opinion. Juergens (1966) in his study of Joseph Pulitzer has drawn attention to the linkage between the sensationalism of this New Journalism and its distinctive prose style claiming it to be slangy, colloquial and personal. His analysis emphasizes that this is one of the chief conduits through which the sensational newspaper was able to communicate its identity to the masses of people who bought it, constructing a language in which readers could identify their own speech patterns and political prejudices. His city-wide network of reporters would scour the city for stories which would fit the paper's pattern: '. . . Pulitzer sent reporters in pursuit of crime, sensation, and disaster stories, and told them to write in a racier narrative style. The headline writers went for punchier verbs and alliteration' (Stevens, 1991: 69).

Campaigns and crusades were a complement to the populist style of the New Journalism allowing self-promotion to act as a key part of its identity and its relationship to its readers. One of the paper's most successful crusades was to raise the funds to construct a base for the Statue of Liberty. In May 1885, the *World* said that since the statue was a gift from the French people to the American people, the people and not the government should build the base. Eight months later, the *World* had collected the necessary $100,000.

William Randolph Hearst: Extending the language of sensation

Competition within the popular newspaper market was to further drive developments in the language of the New Journalism. The most significant moment came when William Randolph Hearst bought the *New York Journal* in 1895. He made the strategic decision to exaggerate all the brasher elements of Pulitzer's approach including an even more prominent set of claims to be on the side of the people and against corruption and complacency in the corridors of power. He had much less of a consistent political agenda than Pulitzer, more rabble-rousing and populist posturing, but in combination with the other features of what became the Yellow Journalism, Hearst's paper was a huge popular success and set new levels of sensation and vulgarity in its language, layout and the blurring of fact and fiction. The *Journal* was a crusading newspaper, too, but it went far beyond other New York newspapers of the time, including Pulitzer's. When the paper secured a court injunction to prevent the sale of a gas franchise, it claimed on 7 July 1897 that what it had discovered was: 'a new idea in journalism'; and it adopted the slogan: 'While Others Talk, the *Journal* Acts' (Mott, 1962: 522–523). Encouraged by circulation success, it continued along this path of public contestation through well-publicized crusades against any sale of a public commodity which it felt was against the interests of the people. It extended this populist concern into alleged political corruption and Hearst then turned to solicit compliments from civic leaders across the country and printed them under such headings as, 'Journalism that Acts; Men of Action in All Walks of Life Heartily Endorse the Journal's Fight in Behalf of the People' (Emery and Emery, 1992: 197).

The *Journal* extended investigative reporting to the extent that the paper itself became involved in solving the Guldensuppe murder case where the reporters were not so much undercover investigators, as going door-to-door in competition with the police in reinforcement of their claims to be servants of the people's interests. And what great claims could be made of this effective publicity stunt in terms of the powers of the newspaper! *Journal* reporters, boasted Hearst, constituted 'a detective force at least as efficient as that maintained at public expense by this or any other city' (*New York Journal*, 28 January 1899) (Mott, 1962: 523–524).

At the culmination of the Guldenseppe murder hunt, the *Journal* devoted 30 columns to the pursuit and capture of the murderer, Thron. A large drawing of his face on page one pointed out his 'cruel mouth and bad eye' The headline on 7 July 1897 again drew attention to the distinctive contribution of this paper to the public good and read:

> NEWS THAT IS NEWS
> The *Journal*, as usual, ACTS While the Representatives of
> Ancient Journalism Sit Idly By and Wait for
> Something to Turn up. (Stevens, 1991: 93)

The shift in the construction of a commercialized popular voice in the American press known as Yellow Journalism emerged in the wake of several factors which were encroaching upon the market for the more conventional popular newspapers of the time. An economic depression and increasing competition from illustrated magazines had led to an intense rivalry to attract and retain readers. Daily newspapers needed to pander still more to the demands of a readership which was becoming more accustomed to having its news packaged in a sensationalized, entertainment format. The journalism which was shaped in this popular daily market set the parameters for the tabloids of the next century with a language and a populist appeal which were shriller, brasher, larger and bolder with screaming headlines and often a reckless disregard for the truth. It was nevertheless a huge commercial success. Between 1880 and 1900 when the yellow press was at its height, it was claimed that these campaigns forged a bond between the language and news values of this style of paper and their putative readerships' common interests: 'The yellows claimed to serve as the arm of the "voiceless masses" in protecting them from the ugly might of the powerful' (Altschull, 1990: 267).

The Spanish-American war of 1896–1898 provided the perfect opportunity for the two main popular New York dailies to rally readers behind a jingoistic celebration of the hostilities in flag-waving fashion. Mott goes so far as to claim that their coverage was directly responsible for the popular fervour which legitimated the government's decision to go to war (Mott, 1962: 527). Both papers drew expertly on the dramatic communicative possibilities of the new style of journalism with its visual impact and powerful delineation of national interests pitted against a starkly negative image of the enemy. This was a concerted and effective exercise in populist propaganda within a democratic society. One genre of story was particularly suited to this campaign, the atrocity story. It had been a familiar feature within broadside and newssheet accounts of wars since the development of commercial printing and had always drawn for its appeal on the twin dynamic of chauvinism and fear of the outsider. Stories of rape, torture and murder were related in graphic detail to an eager audience accompanied with line drawings, and from 1897, their impact was increased by the introduction of half-tone photographs. Stories of Cuban atrocities, clearly predicated on the racialized assumption that such behaviour was a characteristic of the Hispanic peoples, were good for circulation, keeping the readership of both newspapers above the million mark throughout. In one notorious example from this period, the major villain was General Valeriano Weyler, the commander in chief of the Spanish forces in Cuba from early 1896. The Miss Cisneros story combined metaphors of foreign bestiality, personification of the nation and identification with an inno-cent heroine as victim:

> The unspeakable fate to which Weyler has doomed an innocent girl whose only crime is that she has defended herself against a beast in uniform has sent a shiver of horror through the American people. (*New York Journal,* 19 August 1897, quoted in Mott, 1962: 530)

The New Journalism London-style

The New Journalism spread its influence into the British press from America via professional contacts across the Anglophone journalism community. Lee has claimed that it can best be described as a mixture of journalistic and typographical devices, which taken together consti-tuted a new style of journalism, a style which in making the paper more readable, reflected a changing relationship between the newspaper and its readers (Lee, 1976: 121). This reinforces the observation made throughout the book that the form and style of the language of news-papers provide illustrations of shifting social and commercial relationships. Furthermore, these changes came with specific political assumptions. Wiener has observed how the interrelated technical and editorial components of the New Journalism could not be divorced from the democratic assumptions which had enabled it to flourish both commercially and culturally in the United States:

> ... unless the process of Americanization is taken fully into account the democratic component of these changes in the press may be missed. Four key elements of American newspaper culture help to illuminate this crucial transatlantic link between popularization and democratization: speed, informality, human interest, and a combination of access and aggression. (Wiener, 1996: 62)

As economic forces were taking a larger role in determining the development of a viable spread of journalism, it was no coincidence that the New Journalism became crystallized in the practices of the evening London papers as they sought new readers. These papers needed to provide the latest news on their front page to ensure street sales which differentiated them from most of the subscription-based morning press. Inevitably, this competition intensified as cheaper evening newspapers such as the *Pall Mall Gazette* and the *St James' Gazette* reduced their prices from 2 pence to a penny in 1882 and it was in these papers, most notably the *Pall Mall Gazette*, that the newer styles of journalism were introduced as a further commercial ploy to distinguish them from their more sedate morning relations. From 1892, for instance, the *Morning*, a halfpenny London paper, became the first daily newspaper to consistently place news on its front page instead of advertisements.

The innovators: George Newnes and W.T. Stead

Aspects of the American styles of journalism may have already begun to permeate British journalism in the 1860s and 1870s but it was George Newnes who first drew consistently on these stylistic features and adapted them to a British market, testing and creating new boundaries for journalism in a wide range of publications. The first and most influential was, *Titbits from all the interesting Books, Periodicals, and Newspapers of the World*. It was launched as a penny weekly on 22 October 1881 with competitions, statistics, history, bits of news, editorials, correspondence columns, fiction, anecdotes, jokes, legal general knowledge, competitions and adverts. Portraits and interviews with celebrities were also a prominent inclusion in each edition. It was a triumph of promotion, formatting and editorial flair and soon boasted 400,000 to 600,000 weekly sales. Most importantly, he developed a popular community within his paper though a 'sympathetic intimacy' (Jackson, 2000: 13) with his readers which anticipated much of popular journalism's subsequent appeal. There have also been those less appreciative of Newnes' achievements:

> Newnes became aware that the new schooling was creating a class of potential readers – people who had been taught to decipher print without learning much else, and for whom the existing newspapers, with their long articles, long paragraphs, and all-round demands on the intelligence and imagination, were quite unsuited. To give them what he felt they wanted, he started *Tit-Bits*. (Ensor, 1968: 311)

While, on the one hand, this relationship was encapsulated in reformulated style and rhetoric, on the other, it relied on the efficient deployment of technological advances and a commercial sophistication with regard to a relationship between the readers of the newspaper and its advertising. The term New Journalism which became commonplace in Britain from the 1880s, is reputed to have been coined in an uncomplimentary article by Matthew Arnold:

> We have had opportunities of observing a new journalism which a clever and energetic man has lately invented. It has much to recommend it; it is full of ability, novelty, variety, sensation, sympathy, generous instincts; its one great fault is that it is feather-brained. (1887: 638–639)

W.T. Stead, to whose journalism Arnold was referring, was keen for his writing to act as a pressure on the government to bring about change in society based on the agenda of engaged, campaigning journalists. As the assistant editor of the *Pall Mall Gazette* from 1880, and as sole editor from 1883, Stead had introduced scoops, a flair for self-publicity, which drew attention to his newspaper, the development of investigative campaigning journalism in the pursuit of socially progressive causes and the use of emotive and colourful writing. Campaigning, as in the case of Pulitzer and later Hearst, formed an integral element of his desire to form part of a popular momentum for change by leading the people. This is in marked contrast with the later popular journalism of the *Daily Mail* and *Daily Express* and their preference for a more reactive approach to meeting the needs of their readers. In an original interpretation of the old populist adage, *vox populi, vox dei*, Stead set out as part of his journalistic credo that he wanted journalism 'to reproduce in a paper the ideal of God' (Baylen, 1972: 374). His journalism, nevertheless, remained directed towards the liberal middle classes of the metropolis. There was still no sign of the sort of vulgar populism which would come to dominate the American New Journalism and certainly no intention of capturing anything like a mass readership.

Nevertheless, Stead clearly saw the potential of sensationalism to drive a more democratic form of popular involvement:

> It was especially important to Stead that sensationalism, as a journalistic device, facilitate one of the most important 'governing functions' of the press – its 'argus-eyed power of inspection . . .' (Baylen, 1979: 46)

The cross-head was a development he copied from American newspaper practice. In contrast to the dense columns of the morning newspapers, the *Pall Mall Gazette* could be scanned at speed. He included illustrations and line drawings which further broke the monotony of the traditional printed page. He employed specialist commentators to popularize knowledge of contemporary affairs and in his 'Character Sketch' – he blended the interview, word picture and personality analysis. The implications of these changes were clear, making, '. . . the page accessible to less resolute reading at the end of the day and possibly by the family at home' (Brake, 1988: 19).

The development of the interview was again an American import, but Stead deployed it with aplomb in broadening the popular reach of his journalism, conducting his first interview in October 1883, and publishing some 134 of them the following year (Schults, 1972: 63). One major coup was his interview with General Gordon in January 1884 before he embarked for the Sudan. As if to underline the growing importance of women in this era of journalism, Stead's chief interviewer was Hulda Friederichs. Some commentators have located him within a longer tradition of radical journalism:

> Stead's mercurial, hellfire temperament was that of the great pamphleteers. In his boldness and versatility, in his passionate belief in the constructive power of the pen, in so many of his opinions, even in his championship of women, he resembled Daniel Defoe and Jonathan Swift. (Boston, 1990: 101)

The 'Maiden Tribute of Modern Babylon' story published in the *Pall Mall Gazette* from 6 July 1885 synthesized all the ambition of Stead's journalism and campaigning fervour. To highlight the problems of prostitution among young girls, he bought a girl, Liza Armstrong, for £5 to demonstrate how widespread this practice had become and used sensational reporting, eyewitness accounts and interviews to launch his campaign and shame Victorian London into passing a law raising the age of consent. It was a sensation, boosting sales to 100,000. He was eventually imprisoned for 3 months for being judged to have procured the girl as part of his investigative operation but not before he had conducted a nationwide defence of his position and drawn support for his cause from all sections of society. Beyond the technical and stylistic

108

details of what was shortly to be christened the New Journalism, Stead's goal was more a moral and political one. His passionate opposition to the wrongs of society was in keeping with much of the tradition of the 'old corruption' but grafted onto a moral purpose and a well-developed commercial pragmatism. He was a forerunner of a 'journalism of attachment' (Bell, 1997) from a deeply religious perspective. Yet there are those who are more cautious about his sensationalizing of sexual mores and its implications for journalism: '"Sex" had long been a journalistic staple. Stead not only brought it into a "respectable" middle-class paper, he made it central to journalism as political intervention' (Beetham, 1996: 125).

The success of Stead's paper generated a proliferation of penny newspapers in London all attempting to exploit the market for the sort of journalism he had provided and their success undermined the circulation of the *Pall Mall Gazette.* It suffered a further blow when much of his revenue was lost because advertisers were anxious at risking association with the scandalous reputation it had acquired.

Stead, as well as being an innovator, associated with the New Journalism, was an exception within the commercialized discourse of journalism as it widened its scope to broader and more profitable markets to the exclusion of social aims. The polarities within popular journalism are well captured in a communication from one style of editor to another when Newnes wrote to Stead in 1890 on their parting as collaborators on the *Review of Reviews*:

> There is one kind of journalism which directs the affairs of nations; it makes and unmakes cabinets; it upsets governments, builds up Navies and does many other great things. It is magnificent. This is your journalism. There is another kind of journalism which has no such great ambitions. It is content to plod on, year after year, giving wholesome and harmless entertainment to crowds of hardworking people, craving for a little fun and amusement. It is quite humble and unpretentious. This is my journalism. (Friederichs, 1911: 116–117)

Stead had been the journalistic conduit between these two extremes but was redundant once he had served his purpose. Passion had been ousted by the more pragmatic requirements of a commercialized industry. The dividing point at which he stood is well captured in the following:

> The duty of journalism in the first half of the nineteenth century . . . was not to discover the truth. The emphasis was on the polemical power of the writer's pen. Opinion and commentary were the essence of good journalism – except in the recording of parliamentary

activity where accuracy was considered vital . . . By the end of the century technology and commercial need had elevated accuracy and reliability, as well as the ability to meet the daily news deadlines, to the heart of [the] profession of journalism. (Williams, 1998: 54–55)

The *Star*

It was this tension between the altruistic and populist ambitions of journalism which was to shape the continuity of discourses around newspapers to the present. What had started as a consolidation of American-influenced journalistic trends was developed by the daily press in the form of the *Star*. For all Stead's campaigning zeal, his was not a newspaper directed at the masses. He directed his experiments in the New Journalism squarely at the influential middle classes, the decision makers in Victorian England. It was the *Star* which was to rework the new journalistic techniques in order to fashion a mass appeal, which was addressed to the working classes, seeking to combine campaigning with radical social perspectives (Conboy, 2002: 99).

Edited by T.P. O'Connor from 1888–1890, the *Star* was a halfpenny evening paper which was radical in both its politics and its layout and a continuation of the accelerating trends of the New Journalism. O'Connor espoused a brighter method of writing, speed and human interests. He was also aware of the need for journalism to gain attention from the reader in an accelerating world:

> We live in an age of hurry and of multitudinous newspapers . . . To get your ideas across through the hurried eyes into the whirling brains that are employed in the reading of a newspaper there must be no mistake about your meaning: to use a somewhat familiar phrase, you must strike your reader right between the eyes. (O'Connor, 1889: 434)

In its opening number on 17 January 1888, it claimed:

> The STAR will be a radical journal. It will judge all policy – domestic, foreign, social – from the Radical standpoint. This, in other words, means that a policy will be esteemed by us good or bad as it influences for good or evil the lot of the masses of the people . . . In our view, then, the effect of every policy must first be regarded from the standpoint of the workers of the nation, of the poorest and most helpless among them. The charwoman that lives in St Giles, the seamstress that is sweated in Whitechapel, the labourer that stands begging for work outside the dockyard gate . . .

Similar to much of the New Journalism, it was providing shorter news pieces, lively writing, gossip and human interest and had the good fortune in terms of its circulation to be launched in time to exploit the sensation of the Jack the Ripper murders. However, it held out a promise, which seemed to distinguish it from other daily newspapers, delivering all this from a perspective which prioritized the interests and political concerns of the mass of its projected readers. This was a radical departure indeed for the New Journalism as it genuinely attempted to align itself with the lives of its readership and not simply with a rhetorical simulacrum of the language of these readers. On its first day, it sold 142,600 copies and by 1889 its circulation peaked with the Ripper story at 360,598. It was the first genuinely popular daily paper aimed at a mass market but it preceded the market popularization which Harmsworth inaugurated from 1896 with its crucial capitalization via the astute exploitation of advertising on a scale not witnessed before.

The *Star* was politically radical with human interest on a daily basis and with a fresh layout, breaking information up much in the style of the *Answers* and *Tit-bits* but with a different, news-orientated content which distinguished it from these papers. It introduced the Stop Press and lower case type for its cross-heads and lesser headlines. Williams indicates the importance of the role of presentation and layout in the evolving rhetoric of the popular press:

> The essential novelty of the Star is that the new distribution of interest which the second half of the nineteenth century had brought about was now typographically confirmed. From now on the 'New Journalism' began to look what it was. (Williams, 1961: 221)

Goodbody describes the layout thus:

> Headlines often went across two columns, cross-heads were used extensively to break up solid type and leading articles were often intentionally restricted to half a column . . . Later the *Star* used lower case for both secondary headlines and cross-heads, neither of which had been seen in British newspaper typography although they had been widespread in the United states. They also varied the position of broken lines in sub-heads, whereas previously they had been centred. This technique allowed second headlines which summarized the substance rather than pointed to the importance of the article. (Goodbody, 1985: 22)

Above all, journalism in the daily press began to accommodate a more complete range of human experience: '. . . it is the sound principle to which we shall all come at last in literature and journalism, that

111

everything that can be talked about can also be written about' (O'Connor, 1889: 430).

Conclusion

The style of the New Journalism encapsulated the changing relationship between reader and newspaper. Display advertising, sports news, human interest, fast stories transmitted by telegraph, cheap and increasingly visual newspapers, summary leads and front page news all became established in England in the 1890s. Many cheaper weekly publications had introduced some of these features from the 1840s in England but the New Journalism had brought them to a daily readership. The newspapers of the late nineteenth century enabled a new conceptualization of the public as an active, engaged entity and extended that concept through a varied set of strategies which were manifested as letters, editorial identity, leading articles and consumerism targeted through advertising at specific readerships:

> Through the newspaper, readers as well as writers found new ways to communicate. In consequence, it was possible for them to imagine a public, a constituency beyond the individual, the family or the locality, an integrated social whole whose cohesion was underpinned *inter alia* by its access to a common stock of regularly revised knowledge about the world . . . made the nineteenth-century concept of the public possible. (Jones: 202)

There was more sport, crime, entertainment and less politics, all in a livelier style, with more emphasis on human interest and laid out more clearly in an attempt to be more broadly accessible and therefore more profitable. There was also a commercial imperative to cultivate a consistent voice within these papers. Familiarity bred profit. Salmon interprets the way in which the 'discourse of journalism should so insistently declare its personalized character' (Salmon, 29), as inevitable at this point in the commercialization of journalism as a simulacrum standing in for its lack of a relationship with its readers which was in any way as authentic as some of the Radical or Chartist experiments had been or even of the *Times* at the height of its influence with its mid-Victorian upper-middle-class readership. A political irony with implications which continue to resonate within popular journalism today is that as readers were increasingly addressed in a more personal tone about matters which touched the everyday, they were increasingly marginalized in these newspapers from politics (Hampton, 2001: 227).

6 Tabloid talk: Twentieth-century template

Introduction

There were, broadly speaking, two significant shifts in the language of twentieth-century newspapers. The first was the increasing prominence of the sub-editor in constructing a news style, albeit with various institutional preferences, which was able to:

> Combine one story into another, or perhaps combine running reports from several news agencies, a handful of correspondents and half a dozen reporters, to produce a single, intelligible report from a series of confused or even contradictory messages. (Evans, 1972: 7)

This work enabled the development of news as 'a form of knowledge *in itself* not dependent on other discourses to be able to make statements about the world' (Matheson, 2000: 558). Harmsworth's astute arrangement of the news to fit within and around the advertising copy in the *Daily Mail* in plain, easily digested text for the paper's lower-middle-class audience was the first demonstration of this innovation in the status of newspaper language.

The second important shift in the form and scope of newspaper language is the emergence of the tabloid as the most influential sub-genre of journalism of the twentieth century, especially in its elaboration of first, an appeal to a broadly working-class readership and subsequently its incorporation of a more general popular culture. The language and style of first the popular newspaper in Britain and then the tabloid have had an incremental impact on newspapers generally over the last 100 years. Not only have broadsheet newspapers been driven for commercial reasons to adopt a 'compact' format but the emphasis and style of the language of these newspapers have been orientated more towards the news values of the tabloids as these newspapers all try to emphasize their congruence with popular culture in an era of unprecedented competition in the media. It may be, as Bromley and Tumber (1997) have speculated, that after the gradual convergence of tabloid and broadsheet styles, a re-specialization may see different newspapers (particularly in their online manifestations) starting to diverge considerably in their tone, style and coverage once

113

again. Yet from our perspective, the style of tabloid language was certainly the story of the twentieth-century newspaper.

The emergence of a distinctive tabloid idiom indicates a shift in the social parameters of newspaper language. This idiom blends sensation and a calculated disrespect and suspicion of authority, particularly political authority within an overall concentration on the broadest appeal of contemporary popular culture. This chapter will explore the distinctive nature of this sub-genre of newspaper journalism and reflect upon the social implications of its attempts to articulate a populist, media-centric version of contemporary society for a mass readership. It will root the evolution of tabloid newspapers within the general history of popular newspapers and assess the intensification of the rhetoric of social class from the relaunch of the *Daily Mirror* in the 1930s to the reconfiguration of popular Conservatism in the *Sun* as a spokespiece for blue-collar Britain from the 1980s. It will also evaluate the implications of the spread of tabloid features, emphasis and style to elite newspapers as they move to compact formats and, in addition, the adoption of a tabloid ethos by other news media.

New Journalism: Continuities and change

Despite the fact that the popular press of the late Victorian epoch was one which increasingly marginalized the organized political interests of working people, it nevertheless sought to articulate a version of their worldview. This worldview was communicated for commercial reasons to maximize profits through the perfection of an idiom attractive to the widest range of the population. Debates around the impact of the Foster Education Acts of 1870–1871 (Vincent, 1993: 198–199) indicate that there had been readers able and willing to spend a part of their income on published material for decades. They were not new readers – they were a new and profitable readership for a new sort of popular publication. The evolution of the language of newspapers from the New Journalism into the first mass daily newspapers in Britain was above all else a commercial triumph and in particular with its cultural and generic mix, the first manifestation of a properly mass culture.

Most of the popular press in Britain had by the late nineteenth century shifted from a radical culture, drawing upon the collective interests of working people with a view to enable political change, to a cultural expression whose parameters were set by increasingly market-orientated interests which had political as well as economic change securely confined to the accepted tolerances of capitalist markets (Curran, 1978). Despite its more commercialized tone, the popular press had been able to retain an ability to address ordinary people in terms which highlighted subjectivity, entertainment and the traditions of popular miscellany. The production of the new popular newspapers on the cusp of the twentieth century was slicker, their layout made them more visually accessible, their distribution was more regular and they were more attuned to the needs of their advertisers but in all their novelty they still traded upon the longer traditions of popular print culture which had already proved their commercial viability. These publications chose a more effective, dialogic method of control, articulated in terms of reinforcing the political-economic interests of their owners within a set of formulae able to appeal to the widest and most profitable market. Increasingly, this readership was addressed in terms of its commercial potential and its aspirations to middle-class values.

The *Daily Mail*: A commercial language for the masses

The distillation of these trends and strategies in newspaper language and layout came first in a paper which was not tabloid at all. In fact, it was rather a dignified publication, unsensationalist, with advertisements on the front page to emphasize its respectability and certainly with no taint of political radicalism. Yet it was the *Daily Mail* which created the mass market for newspapers which would set the cultural scene which would enable the tabloid papers to later extend the experiment with the language of popular appeal. On 4 May 1896, the *Daily Mail* was launched as a reader-friendly morning paper aimed at a class of readers not yet attracted by the daily press. It was priced at a halfpenny and aimed at the lower middle classes, shop workers, secretarial staff, office workers, clerks and, as its greatest novelty, women readers. It has been observed that Harmsworth knew from personal experience that there was a broader interest in a news agenda beyond the narrow traditions of political newspapers:

> He knew it was also what people talked about in the kitchen, parlour, drawing room, and over the garden wall; namely, other people – their failures and successes, their joys and sorrows, their money and their food, their peccadilloes. The Daily Mail was thus the first to cater for women readers. (Graves and Hodge, 1971: 55)

This female orientation was achieved by including more material which imitated the print culture which had been demonstrably popular with women readers since the early nineteenth century – the weekly magazine. The *Mail*'s daily magazine which included a specific Women's

Column soon expanded to a whole page. Woman's World in an early experimental edition of the paper on Saturday, 22 February 1896 included:

> When Love Begins to Wane; Sponge Cake; What do your eyes say?
> Fortune Telling Teacups; The Jewel For Each Month; Your Character From Handwriting.

The *Daily Mail*'s main change was the way in which it shaped the newspaper's content to fit the space available. Its captions allowed the gist of an article to be taken in at a glance and the brevity of the pieces added to the overall impression of space in composition and variety in content. The language of this journalism needed to be made to fit the new layout and compartmentalization of stories which meant that the role of the sub-editor was of paramount importance; copy had to be pruned and adapted to fit within the space between the illustration, headlines and advertising. However, the tight control of length of item and the cutting of stories to fit space also enabled opinion to be more subtly incorporated into the editorial process through the language structure thus increasing the possibility of 'slanting the news by emphasis or omission to suit the political views of the proprietor' (Clarke, 2004: 265).

Its advertising slogan in the early days was a call to an ambition for cut-price self-improvement characteristic of the epoch and the class of its readers:

THE PENNY PAPER FOR A HALFPENNY

Having learned from the profitable publishing experience of Newnes, for whom Harmsworth had worked in his early days as a freelance contributor to *Tit-Bits*, and backed by the fortune he had amassed through his *Answers to Correspondents* with the addition of a keen appreciation of the importance of the link between advertising, capital investment and circulation, the new paper was an immediate commercial success. He had also learnt from the ways in which the *Star* had been able to appeal by its concentration on the lighter aspects of life but had jettisoned its radical politics. Popular appeal was to be articulated as commercial momentum not as the platform for radical reform. By 1900 its circulation had almost reached the million mark and the era of the mass-circulation daily newspaper had arrived in Britain.

Its first leader encapsulates the appeal of this combination of technology, value for money and a well-identified readership:

> . . . the note of the *Daily Mail* is not so much economy of price as conciseness and compactness. It is essentially the busy man's paper . . . Our stereotyping arrangements, engines, and machines are of the latest English and American construction, and it is the use of

these inventions on a scale unprecedented in any English newspaper office that enables the *Daily Mail* to effect a saving of from 30
to 50 per cent, and to be sold for half the price of its competitors.

The newspaper was presented as being not cheap but a bargain. It was
conservative in its politics and layout, with advertisements on the front
page and was ideal for the commuter. The short articles, clearly laid
out, were written in order to have a breadth of appeal – a commercial as
well as a textual achievement and one which became a hallmark of the
construction of this type of popularity. The front page of the *Daily Mail*
came to include regular, light items such as GOSSIP OF THE DAY, OUR
SHORT STORY, SOME INTERESTING ITEMS, LAST LOOK ROUND
and was traditional to the extent that it did not focus heavily on news.
The reports from the London Courts on page 3 entitled, ON THE SEAMY
SIDE are a direct continuation of the tradition of *Cleave's Weekly Police
Gazette* and other Sunday papers. Fashions, the personalities behind
the news, a more conversationally based style of news were all features
of Harmsworth's appropriation of the style and content of the New
Journalism. It complemented its commercial appeal with an influential
form of populist chauvinism combining in Engel's words: 'triumphalism
. . . xenophobia . . . and, of course, crime . . . in about equal proportions'
(Engel, 1996: 60). This reached an early peak during the Boer War
(1899–1902). It placed itself at the centre of popular enthusiasms and
events such as Exhibitions, the relief of Mafeking in the Boer War and
Royal events. The Queen's Diamond Jubilee was celebrated on 23 June
1897 and was feted by none in more effusive patriotic terms than the
Daily Mail's eulogy:

> We ought to be a proud nation today, proud of our fathers who
> founded this empire, proud of ourselves who have kept and
> increased it, proud of our sons, whom we can trust to keep what we
> hand down and increase it for their sons.

Catherine Hughes (Hughes, 1986: 187) has argued that it was the speed
of production, distribution and reaction to popular opinion which
began to unravel the more sedate cultural patterns of the previous era,
following popular impulses and threading new patterns around narratives of empire and the place of the people in that project. It was this
new form of the mass popular newspaper which for the first time, on a
daily basis, was incorporating the people as readers into the imperial
project within a technologically influenced stylistics which came to
maturity in the material presentation of this newspaper. Harmsworth
was first to conceive the idea of a mass-circulation daily, 'to bring the
proud and vital spirit of empire to the breakfast tables of the queen's
fiercely loyal, lower-middle-class subjects (Hughes, 1986: 200). National

narratives were commercially attractive to a newspaper aiming for a nation-wide audience bolstered in its self-regard by association with empire and the possession of overseas territories again exemplified in an early prototype:

> OUR BIRTHDAY
>
> Four hundred years ago today the foundation stone of the British Empire was laid On March 5 1496, Henry VII granted the petition of John Cabot and his three sons, of Bristol, and on the same day the Privy Seal was attached to a charter granting these four bold mariners liberty to hoist the English flag on shores hitherto unknown to Christian people, and to acquire the sovereignty of them for England . . . Today that flag flutters in the eye of the sun at every hour of his endless march from day to day, and bounds have been set to the British Empire by the limitations of terrestrial space . . . That England has done so well in the race for empire, and has secured the pick of colonial locations all over the world is due to the fact that we started early and worked manfully before Europe had grown too big for its peoples, and for this our race may thank the hardy pioneers whose charter we commemorate today. (5 March 1896)

The commonsensical, low-key populism of the new newspaper was to be modelled on the conversational intimacy modelled on Newnes's journalism (Campbell, 2001) which in turn was a direct appropriation, for a British market, of the commercialized popular idiom from America. This conversational tone can be illustrated by reference to a report on a meeting with a man recently back from the Cape province which on 21 February 1896 ran under the following heading:

> Is Kruger Toppling?
> A Chat with an Englishman just returned from Johannesburg

Goodbody has suggested that in terms of targeting a popular readership, Harmsworth: '. . . did not lead or follow the public mood, he accompanied it' (Goodbody, 1985: 24) and this certainly matches the longer term trend within the language of popular newspapers observed by Hampton (2004) in the shift from an emphasis on education to the representation of increasingly well-defined and commercially targeted readers.

Despite the fact that Harmsworth's revolution had not been a tabloid one, he was instrumental in the development of the new format. Harmsworth and Pulitzer collaborated on producing a one-off tabloid edition of the New York *World* on 1 January 1901. Its 32 pages were half the size of the normal newspaper. Its joint editors dubbed it a 'tabloid' newspaper and heralded it presciently as the 'newspaper of the twentieth century' (Mott, 1962: 666–667). In 1903, Harmsworth launched his own *Daily Mirror* in a tabloid format but one with a specific appeal to women readers. Unlike later experiments with the genre, it was not to prove a success in this guise. The success of the *Daily Mail* triggered the appearance of a rival in the *Daily Express* from 1900 which consistently concentrated the American novelty of news on the first page for the first time successfully in a British mass-market daily morning newspaper from 1901, after the incorporation of the *Morning* which had championed this format, and which drew on the expertise of expatriate American Blumenfeld: 'grafting my American branch on the British oak' (Blumenfeld, 1944: 102–112). Arthur Pearson's instruction to his journalists on the *Daily Express*, to 'never forget the cabman's wife', was executed by Blumenfeld who became a forceful interpreter of American methods to a nation still genuinely reluctant to seize the bit (Wiener, 1996: 72–73).

The story of the popular newspaper in Britain in the period up to the outbreak of World War II is a fascinating manifestation of the way in which a popular rhetoric developed through the competing efforts of four daily newspapers to attract and keep an increasing share of readers and to inspire them with their particular version of popular reality. The developments of the 1930s can be categorized as part of the continuum that was the New Journalism; perfecting the pattern of a commercially attractive popular journalism. The 1930s was the defining decade for the direction of popular daily newspapers in Britain. It was the period of greatest expansion in terms of sales and readers and of the commercialization of the popular newspaper markets. The popular daily press of this period also successfully assimilated two traditional English newspaper formats – the illustrated newspaper and the popular Sunday paper (Williams, 1961: 231).

The *Daily Herald*: A left-leaning alternative

The only popular paper which steered away from a commercially dominated course until the 1930s was the *Daily Herald* which had started as a strike sheet founded by print workers in 1911 and had been turned into a daily newspaper supporting the position of the Trades Unions in 1912 by George Lansbury and Ben Tillett. In 1922, it was taken over by the Trades Union Congress (TUC). The *Herald* was, according to Bingham (2004), dedicated to expounding the 'workers' perspective' against the 'dope' peddled by the 'capitalist press' (Bingham, 2004: 42).

The paper was relaunched on 17 March 1930 and its circulation grew almost immediately from a quarter of a million to a million, beginning to rival the 'big two', the *Daily Express* and the *Daily Mail*. Reporting its own success in its initial offer for a renewed and extensive version of insurance for subscribers, it claimed:

> RUSH TO REGISTER FOR £10,000 INSURANCE
> DAILY HERALD SCHEME WITH BENEFITS FOR ALL. (18 March 1930)

The conditions of the *Herald*'s sale to Odhams Press included a continued commitment to TUC perspectives so that the new version of the newspaper contained explicit calls to the tradition of Labour and Trades Union politics in the press and attempts to forge a solidarity with its readers based on its adherence to that tradition:

> FORWARD!
> Today the 'Daily Herald' appears in a new suit. The spirit and purpose behind it remain unchanged.
> For years we have been the official exponent of the views of the great British Labour and Trade Union Movement. That high position we are proud to hold today . . .
> We say to our readers old and new. Here is *your* newspaper. Much has been done in the past. A great deal lies ahead. Let us march. (17 March 1930)

Its political message was often uncompromising and written from such a clear Socialist perspective of political involvement that it constituted a radically different choice to any of its daily popular competitors:

> DISCIPLINE
> We print today a letter from Mr Josiah Wedgewood, M.P. on the burning issue of discipline in the Parliamentary Labour Party. But we find it somewhat hard to discover what it is that he recommends.
> What are the limits of individual liberty within an organised Party whose very existence depends on loyalty and discipline?
> This is no abstract question, no plaything for theorists. It is vital and urgent, primary and ultimate.
> On the answer to it depends the survival of the Labour Government and that whole complex of social progress for which the government stands. (25 March 1930)

Its great skill included being able to take features which had become popularized in the daily press of the early century and give them a slant which tilted them more towards a politically engaged viewpoint. This is illustrated by the use of medical opinion on the condition of factory workers in an opinion column which calls on the expert opinion of Dr Marion Phillips:

> TALKING IT OVER
> Where the Sun is Shut Out!
> Factory Workers Who Miss Tonic of Spring. (23 March 1930)

The stress of many of its rags-to-riches stories was on the ordinariness of the recipients of good fortune and sometimes, more interestingly, in a departure from the melodramatic interventions of fate, these stories contained potential for individuals to improve their lot through hard work in a meritocratic society:

> PROMOTION FROM THE LOWER DECK
> REAL CHANCES FOR EVERY BOY
> How to open still wider the road to promotion for all classes in the
> Navy is to be examined by the Admiralty. (24 March 1930)

There remained also an element of the sensationalist exotica of the day on offer in its rivals:

> The Truth Behind the Dope Peril By G. W. L. Day
> WORLD-WIDE DRUG SYNDICATES
> POISON FLOOD (18 March 1930)

A selection of front-page headlines indicate a distinctive set of news values even at this time of intensifying competition with the *Daily Express* and *Daily Mail*:

> **THE TRUTH BEHIND THE DEARER BACON PRICES SCANDAL**
> **FOREIGN EXPORTERS POCKET £5,000,000** (23 August 1930)

> **MINERS SHOT FOR THE ROOSEVELT CODE**
> ***Men Strike to Assert Their Right To Organise***
> **WOMEN GASSED AND MAN KILLED**
> **OWNERS' GANGS FIRE ON STRIKERS** (2 August 1930)

The Daily Mail: Responding to competition

The *Daily Mail* did not want to be left out in the race to improve its visual attractiveness to the expanding reading public. It too considered that the new potential of typographic developments and illustration needed to be harnessed to the continuing tradition of the newspaper's popular appeal. There were many aspects of the paper, which, despite its new livery, were rooted in its traditional set of values and the characteristic tone of appeal to its particular mass readership. Its slogan, for example, remained 'For King and Empire', boasting its profoundly loyalist and imperial perspectives. The paper still promoted itself as the 'world's greatest advertising medium' and as if to reinforce that claim, it still persevered with a predominance of advertising on its first page. The sections: 'Looking at Life' and 'Court and Society' were aspirational in tone. Its appeal to women was as strong as before and was based on the successful and popular formula of questions and answers on dress, cookery, children and the nursery, beauty, housewifery in a daily feature entitled,

'DAILY MAIL' WOMEN'S BUREAU

The relaunch of the *Daily Express*

The *Daily Express* did not, in its response, attempt to target a specific social class. There seemed to be little call for such a product as there was clearly still mileage for editorial and advertisers in trying to provide a more general cross-class appeal, drawing upon American precedents. Arthur Christiansen, the editor of the *Daily Express* in its most successful era between 1933 and 1957, required that news reports should be accessible to the whole spectrum of society:

> I tried to simplify news in such a way that it would be interesting to the permanent secretary of the Foreign office and to the charwoman who brushed his office floor in the morning. (Christiansen, 1961: 147)

The summer of 1933 marked a significant breakthrough in popular newspapers in Britain with editor Christiansen's revolutionary matching of layout to the broader popular agenda in the *Daily Express*. He produced a paper with cleaner print, which was better spaced, had more and bigger headlines and cross-headings to break up the page into more accessible sections. This was the turning point – accessibility. The new typography and layout constituted as important a part of popular rhetoric as the content of the newspaper or the language in which it was couched. The catalogue of popular disaster and crime which had remained a staple of popular print culture is well represented here but in a much more attractive layout, inviting the eye to peruse the headlines and catch more of the story at a glance:

Girl 'Duellist' On Stiletto Death
BOY SHOWN TRICK OF STABBING
SHE OFFERS HER BLOOD FOR HIM – TOO LATE (22 August 1933)

Unemployment, a major feature of the time, makes its way into the paper on 22 August 1933. The front page announces that this will be a series of articles looking at the issue from the inside:

What Do The Unemployed Think? – 1
A WORKLESS MAN LAYS BARE HIS SOUL

However, this is a sentimental account relying on the New Journalism's subjective interview techniques to bring the issue of unemployment to the fore. It steers clear of radical solutions and displays in the person of the unemployed man, a scepticism of those in power. Ultimately it is a philanthropic and rather defeatist attitude which lingers in the mind. The issue is raised but the causes of mass unemployment and the political solutions to the problem take second place to the rather maudlin, sensationalized representation of the 'workless man'. This version of popular journalism was able to fashion an escapist version of reality to counter much of the gloom of the period. At the same time as mass unemployment threatened increasing numbers of ordinary people, the *Daily Express* was highlighting coverage of the glamour and sensation of high-society in William Hickey's gossip column: 'These Names Make NEWS'.

The *Daily Express* was rapidly becoming the perfect contemporary vehicle for portraying the news of the day and a great deal else beside in a language and format accessible to the general reader. The world of the economic depression in Europe was not closely scrutinized. The gaze of the reader was distracted elsewhere into the miscellany of popular escapism. The status quo was fine by the *Daily Express* and it appeared to go along with the notion that the world was in the safe hands of trusted politicians and businessmen. It also had little truck with radical solutions and presented the ordinary reader with an assertive view of the middle-class aspirations of working people.

The *Daily Mirror*: Commercializing the working classes

For all the success of these papers in attracting the broadest range of lower-middle-class popular readers, it was the *Daily Mirror* which was to define and then dominate the tabloid market with a language of specifically proletarian appeal (Bingham and Conboy, 2009). By 1934 the circulation of the *Daily Mirror* was falling towards an unacceptably low 700,000. Its readers were predominantly the metropolitan, middle class who might be better served by the *Express* and the *Mail*: 'retired colonels, dowagers, professional gentlemen and schoolmistresses' . . . Cudlipp called it the '*Daily Sedative*' (Cudlipp, 1953: 64). It was decided that something had to be done to revive the financial fortunes of the newspaper within an increasingly competitive popular market. It had been identified that there was an imbalance with more right-wing newspapers than the market could sustain (Pugh, 1998: 426). Furthermore, the existing left-of-centre newspapers consisted of more serious-minded and party affiliated publications such as the *Daily Herald, Daily Worker* and the Liberal *News Chronicle*. A newspaper which could encompass a broader appeal to a working-class audience and spice it up with

123

entertainment, humour and engagement with the lived experiences of readers could find a vacant position in the market. The success of the relaunched *Daily Mirror* was built on a formula based on two American tabloids, the New York *Daily Mirror* and *Daily News*, skilfully adapted to a British cultural context and combined with the advice of an American advertising agency, J. Walter Thompson. The old Northcliffe formula of the telegraphic sentence was deployed in a modern layout (Edelman, 1966: 40). The guiding light behind this was its editorial director Harry Guy Bartholomew who introduced the heavy black type, which was to distinguish the *Mirror* from all its competitors from his first year in charge. Its 'Tabloid Revolution' of 1934–1937 had begun but it still needed to find an authentic voice to match its bold appearance. Engel has described its new-found appeal under his stewardship in the following terms:

> In the fuggy atmosphere of a bare-floored pre-war pub, the *Mirror* was the intelligent chap leaning on the counter of the bar: not lah-di-dah or anything – he liked a laugh, and he definitely had an eye for the girls – but talking a lot of common sense. (Engel, 1996: 161)

It soon began to pick up in terms of circulation but it was the crucial factor of its identity, its ambition to articulate the broad interests of the working classes, which was to take longer to develop. Edelman has tried to capture something of the man trusted with expressing that identity:

> Though the 'Establishment' was still an object of reverence, 'Bart', as everyone called him, was against it. Long before the aristocracy and its imitators in Britain recognized that their authority was crumbling, Bart spontaneously pointed out to the millions of working-class and lower middle-class readers of the *Mirror* that they mattered, that many of the old accepted and snobbish values were bunk, that stuffed prigs should not be taken at their self-assessment, and that you didn't have to be a public school man to have worthwhile views. (Edelman, 1966: 38)

It became a daily popular newspaper which articulated the views and aspirations of the working classes and perfected a vernacular style which transmitted that solidarity even if it was in an intensely commercialized form. A key element in this construction of a working-class voice was the use of letters such as 'Viewpoint', 'Live Letters', 'Star letter' and later the 'Old Codgers' replies to these letters as a barometer of readers' views. Also key to its development of a demotic printed language, were the columns of Cassandra (William Connor) who provided an abrasive, populist political edge which railed against unemployment and appeasement and the complacency of the ruling classes in a language able to provoke debate and stir up passions.

The sensationalist headline which Christiansen had done much to develop in the broadsheet *Daily Express* was to be extended by this language into a weapon of both sensation and later popular indignation. Headlines of the 1930s which Cudlipp himself recalls penning include those which were characteristic of the new edge to the tabloid journalism of the *Daily Mirror* in the 1930s:

> **I AM THE WOMAN YOU PITY**
> **REVELLER VANISHES FOR DAYS -**
> **COMES BACK AS POP-EYED DRAGON**
> **SHOUTING 'WHOOPEE! WHAT A NIGHT!'** (Cudlipp, 1953: 80)

Capturing the voice of the people

It was during World War II that the *Daily Mirror* was able to take up the mantle as spokesperson of the ordinary people with a hunger for radical change in favour of their interests and against the damaging social and political complacencies of the pre-war era. Without hyperbole, Cudlipp can claim that it became: '. . . the newspaper of the masses, the Bible of the Services' rank and file, the factory worker and the housewife' (1953: 136).

In the words of historian A.J.P. Taylor it constituted a:

> . . . serious organ of democratic opinion [which] gave an indication as never before what ordinary people in the most ordinary sense were thinking. The English people at last found their voice. (Taylor, 1976: 548–549)

Much of its credibility was derived, in the early war years, from the astute identification of the inefficiencies of the bureaucrats and their hindrance of the war effort. Cassandra's crusade against 'Army foolery', for instance, managed to continually strike a popular chord which was patriotic at the same time as it was disturbing for the wartime leaders. He carried it off because the readers genuinely recognized the problems which he identified in the many cosy preconceptions of hierarchy and protocol in British society. In stark contrast to much of the conservative individualism of populist appeal in the press of the 1930s or the sublimation of workers into the imperial effort, there is a decisive shift to a collective and a working-class perspective in the *Daily Mirror*. On 11 May 1945 it adopted the slogan:

FORWARD WITH THE PEOPLE

This emphasis culminated in its coverage of the lead-up to voting in the 1945 General Election. In a stroke of populist genius, the paper began a campaign of power and subtlety – not mentioning the name of the

125

Labour party but focusing on the experiences and memories of ordinary people as a repository of folk memory. The catch-phrase was memorable and convincing:

I'LL VOTE FOR HIM (5 June 1945)

The people and the nation are merged in a vision of radical change for the benefit of both. An editorial on July 4 reads:

THE ONE OR THE MANY
... When people all over the country go to the polls tomorrow **for whom will they be voting?** Not for this party or that, not for one leader as against another, not to express appreciation or gratitude. They will be voting for **themselves**. They will be voting to express confidence in their own view of the kind of world they desire to live in. They will be voting for the policies which they believe are likely to bring such a world into existence. This election is a **national** issue, not a personal one.

Post 1945, the *Daily Mirror* continued to articulate the aspirations of the class of reader which had emerged from the war with a strong sense of social solidarity and a determination that things would change to the benefit of the ordinary people. At this point, only the *Daily Mirror* and the *Daily Sketch* were technically tabloids but the style had been gaining in influence since the 1930s in the popular market. Popular journalism with the *Daily Mirror* comes to mean a combination of style (including layout) – mass circulation – and address (rhetorical/content) as never before. The *Daily Mirror* with its astute identification of a representational style and above all the voice to match that constituency was to continue to play a key part is that evolution through the 1950s as it overtook the *Daily Express* in 1949 and by 1967 had reached the still unmatched pinnacle of 5.25 million daily sales (Tunstall, 1996: 43–45).

Its continued success was rooted in the 'successful projection of personality' of which Fairlie wrote in 1957 describing the 'Old Codgers' section of the letters page:

No other feature in British journalism so superbly creates the atmosphere of a public bar, in which everyone sits cosily round the scrubbed deal tables, arguing the toss about anything which happens to crop up, while the Old Codgers buy pints of mixed for the dads, and ports and lemon for the dear old mums. (Fairlie, 1957: 11)

Bolam as editor of *Mirror* (1948–1953) staked a claim for the linkage of sensation and public service, which continues to inform much of the popular tabloids' self-image (Rhoufari, 2000; Deuze, 2005):

We believe in the sensational presentation of news and views, as a necessary and valuable public service ... Sensationalism does not

mean distorting the truth. It means the vivid and dramatic presentation of events so as to give them a forceful impact on the mind of the
reader. It means big headlines, vigorous writing, simplification into
familiar everyday language, and the wide use of illustration by
cartoon and photograph. (*Daily Mirror*, 30 July 1949: 1)

From 1953, Cudlipp was editor-in-chief and editorial director of both
Mirror and Pictorial; according to Geoffrey Goodman, he transformed
'the feelings, attitudes, beliefs, prejudices, romantic aspirations and
illusions, nostalgic dreams and awkward-squad absurditites of the
postwar masses into a kind of national common currency' (Greenslade,
2003: 59). Yet, the language which it used to maintain coherence in
this articulation of its readership into the 1950s and 1960s has been
criticized by Smith as having 'stylized working class language into
parody . . .' (Smith, 1975: 238) and he was not alone in decrying the
popular press as culpable in a cultural drift from authentic representation of the voice and interest of the working classes. Richard Hoggart's
Uses of Literacy denounced a sensational, sex and entertainment-
obsessed popular press for its part in destroying a serious working-class
culture sustained by the 'old broad-sheets' (Hoggart, 1958).

The *Sun*: A blue-collar vernacular for the new right

The most significant, recent development in the history of British
tabloid newspapers was the relaunch of the *Sun* in 1969. Thomas has
summarized the epoch-defining pitch for a new, downmarket popular
newspaper in Murdoch's conviction that the *Mirror* had become too
highbrow for its readers by the 1960s and, with former *Daily Mirror* journalist Larry Lamb, he set out to produce an alternative that was explicitly
based on an updated version of their rival's irreverent approach of previous decades (Thomas, 2005: 72). The *Sun* targeted younger readers,
dropped the serious ambition of the *Mirror*, embraced the permissiveness
of the age and provided a disrespectful, anti-establishment, entertain-
ment-driven agenda. It reinforced its popular credentials by exploiting
television advertising and an intensified interest in the off and on-screen
activities of the characters in soap operas on British television. Greenslade
has summed up its impact in the following overview:

> . . . the *Sun* had shown that there was an audience for softer, fea-
> tures-based material and heavily angled news in which comment
> and reporting were intertwined. It also adopted a more idiosyn-
> cratic agenda, presenting offbeat stories that fell outside the remit of
> broadcast news producers. It cultivated brashness, deliberately
> appealing to the earthier interests – and possibly, baser instincts –
> of a mass working-class audience. (Greenslade, 2003: 337)

127

It was the ability of the *Sun* to transform the language of populist appeal away from the *Mirror*'s left-leaning progressive brand of politics to a new articulation of the sentiments and policies of the right which provided the *Sun* with its trump card, employing Walter Terry, former political editor of the right-wing *Daily Mail*, and Ronnie Spark to provide a demotic language to shape the editorial ambition for Murdoch/Lamb's shift to the right in 1978. In the 1970s and 1980s the Tories gained the support of the *Sun* (Negrine: 1994) which had become synchronized with the aspirations and identities of the classes which had been credited with the swing to Thatcher in the 1979 election. This represented an astute mapping of the newspaper's idiom onto the hegemonic shift to the ideological project of the Conservative Party in government. Its effect was contagious to many areas of the press, with its rabid anti-union stance becoming a perspective maintained by most of the national newspaper press (Marr, 2005: 169). It soon perfected a style of vernacular address which highlighted the perceived interests of a newly empowered blue-collar conservatism. This was however nothing new: 'Ever since its birth, the popular press has bolstered capitalism by encouraging acquisitive, materialistic and individualistic values' (Seymour-Ure, 2000: 23).

Kelvin MacKenzie, the editor from 1981 encapsulated this new mood perfectly. His preferred slogan was 'Shock and Amaze on Every Page' (Chippendale and Horrie, 1992: 332) as he displayed bombastic and hyperbolic language on all aspects of life in Britain and beyond. Fiercely patriotic and a staunch supporter of the Conservative Prime Minister, he was always unequivocally supportive of British military involvement. This was demonstrated most infamously by its jingoistic coverage in the Falklands: 'GOTCHA: Our lads sink gunboat and hole cruiser' (4 May 1982). The paper adopted 'Maggie', feted British soldiers as 'our boys' and ran front-page headlines redolent of popular speech as never before: SCUM OF THE EARTH – KINNOCK'S PARTY OF PLONKERS – SUPERSTAR MAGGIE IS A WOW AT WEMBLEY – 70, 80, 90 PHEW WOT A SCORCHER! It was, furthermore, able to extend itself into more extreme examples of parody for its amused readership and in the process possibly contributed to a more general process of political trivialization:

WHY I'M BACKING KINNOCK, BY STALIN (*Sun*, 1 June 1987)

Finding a language for sexuality

Changing times had brought with them changing attitudes to public discussions of sexuality. The *Sun* managed to articulate the resonance of Hunt's 'permissive populism' (1998) of the 1970s and 1980s. Once the veneer of didacticism had been stripped away (Bingham, 2009), public discussion of the direct and vicarious pleasures of sexuality became commonplace within a language of vulgar celebration best epitomized by the descriptions of the Page 3 Girl – 'Cor!'; 'Wot a Scorcher!'; 'Stunner!'. It provided a language appealing to women as part of a broader celebration of heterosexual pleasure for ordinary people. 'We Enjoy Life and We Want You To Enjoy It With Us' announced the first 'Pacesetters' section for women (*Sun,* 17 November 1969: 14). Holland (1983) has provided a subtle reading of how the news agenda of the paper and its raucous appeal formed part of a linguistic endorsement of the power of pleasure in the lives of working-class readers, presenting itself as the champion of sexual liberation albeit of a particularly narrow, heterosexual, male-dominated variety.

This sexualization of the language of what soon became the most popular and most influential newspaper in Britain became even more pronounced in a more intensely competitive market. It seemed as if, as Snoddy has discussed (1992), the race was on to find the bottom of the barrel in terms of public tolerance. The *Daily Star*, launched in 1978, beat the *Sun* by a short head in the plummet towards the lowest tolerance point in the late 1980s in the sexualization of popular culture (Holland, 1998). It attempted to provide the *Sun* with its nemesis but it failed and has been described as having, 'a circus layout that fairly burst from the pages . . . the paper used more italics, more reverses, and more graphics in conjunction with sensational heads and stories to give a sense of excitement and power' (Taylor, 1992: 45). Its limited success meant that with sales falling and advertisers withdrawing contracts by the early 1990s, the paper withdrew from its policy of 'bonk journalism', thus demonstrating that continuous coarsening of their language does not guarantee success for the next generation of popular newspapers.

Declining deference: Royalty

The diminishing deference within British society in the postwar era was perfectly articulated in the popular press, especially the tabloids and this found early expression in attitudes to the monarchy. A greater aggressiveness in royal journalism was first demonstrated in the matter of Princess Margaret's relationship with Peter Townsend. On 14 June 1953 a particularly controversial headline captured the new-found assertiveness of the popular newspaper to the royal family when the *Daily Mirror* urged: 'Come On Margaret! Please make Up Your Mind' (19 August 1953). At least they said, 'please' at this point!

129

The *Daily Mirror* ran a poll on whether Princess Margaret and Townsend should marry or not and the Press Council was hugely critical of the paper's coverage as were conservative newspapers such as the *Times* and the *Daily Telegraph* but there was no going back. As a supplement to this in the 1970s, the romantic saga of Prince Charles's courtships were to provide the first sustained taste of the new lack of deference towards the monarchy. The stories peaked in the 1990s with the colourful and controversial adventures of Diana, Princess of Wales, but there were still notable stories beyond the 1990s as tabloids became more desperate than ever to milk Royal scandal or even fabricate it to boost sales such as in the 'Spy in the Palace' coup by the *Daily Mirror* and the Burrell affair (Coward, 2007).

Tabloidization: The permeation of the popular

We may consider that the list of trends associated with tabloidization constitutes the newspaper's major contemporary alteration. Yet no matter how great the impact of the tabloid style has been in the popular press, it is in the migration of its characteristics to other media where it continues to have greatest relevance to contemporary debates. Tabloidization may refer to an increase in news about celebrities, entertainment, lifestyle features, personal issues, an increase in sensationalism, in the use of pictures and sloganized headlines, vulgar language and a decrease in international news, public affairs news including politics, the reduction in the length of words in a story and the reduction of the complexity of language and also a convergence with agendas of popular and in particular television culture. It is clearly, if nothing else, a composite growl-list of elements, some of which have haunted the minds of commentators on journalism over centuries. It is because of this lack of specificity that Sparks (2000) questions whether tabloidization is a useful diagnostic tool at all but he does concede that the debate itself is an indication of a specifically contemporary set of worries over the nature of journalism across media. Popular tabloid newspapers are primarily constructed through a combination of format and language: 'editorial matter is presented in emotive language in easy-to-consume formats' (Rooney, 2000: 91). Tabloid tendencies to sensationalize headlines and to cross-reference celebrity and entertainment issues can increasingly be seen in the elite press and other news media as an attempt to reach new audiences in a crowded market and a changing cultural environment.

The first trend within tabloidization is the literal transformation of broadsheets to tabloid format; from *Mail* in 1971 to the *Independent* in

2003. The second is the spread of the tabloid style and news values to the elite press. McLachlan and Golding (2000) chart that the growth in visuals in relation to text is one indicator of tabloidization, squeezing text out of the frame. Bromley observed this trend as it gathered momentum through the 1990s:

> At first, the 'quality' press ignored the substantive issues of tabloid news; then decried them. These papers . . . subsequently began reporting and commenting on the behaviour of the tabloid press, which led to the vicarious reporting of the issues themselves. Finally, the broadsheet papers, too, carried the same news items. (1998: 31)

Thomas (2005) argues that there is a direct connection between aspects of the development of tabloid newspapers' language and their reporting of politics which has drifted into the elite press especially as they have increasingly depended on the populist techniques of the tabloids to maintain their place in an increasingly competitive market. This has meant a move away from balanced reporting, positive, politician-centred propaganda to a more negative, journalist-dominated approach and to one-story front pages, screaming headlines and short, punchy campaigning prose at the expense of more detailed text or long quotations from politicians. In this sense, Thomas claims, the tabloid medium certainly has affected the message, and has arguably impacted not just on the popular press but the wider reporting culture as well (Thomas, 2005: 154–155).

Readers have become more than ever constructed by the newspapers in terms of consumerism than active engagement in politics (McGuigan, 1993: 178) meaning that political news has become simply another part of the scandal/entertainment industry (Franklin, 1997 2004) and a glance at the activities and sound-bite oriented reporting of the mainstream television news channels shows the extent to which the 'reductive language' (Seymour-Ure, 1996: 222) of the popular tabloids have migrated. Fairclough (1995b) and Fowler (1991) observe a movement in news media towards what they term a 'conversationalisation' of public language including political language while Marr concludes that the consequent tone of mocking scepticism adopted almost as a contemporary default has eroded the credibility of democracy (Marr, 2005: 71).

Yet the influence of tabloid techniques on the language of the elite press has not been uniformly negative, as Greenslade implies when praising the success of the editor of the *Guardian* from the 1970s in appealing to a young, professional readership:

> The key to Preston's success stemmed in part from his subtle adoption and adaptation of tabloid techniques. He realised the importance

> of 'selling' the stories, the virtues of brevity and the benefits of
> being proactive in both news-gathering and features selection.
> (Greenslade, 2003: 428)

Rusbridger (2005) has highlighted that the future of the quality press
will be determined in large part by the way that it responds to the pressures of the commercialized, tabloidized market and McNair sees
changes in the content and style of the elite press as a positive move
towards a more inclusive even democratic culture: 'Less pompous, less
pedagogic, less male, more human, more vivacious, more demotic'
(McNair, 2003: 50).

The third characteristic is the crossover of tabloid style and news
values to other media.

As the tabloid newspapers decline in direct sales they are nevertheless, and perhaps this in part explains their slow demise, exporting
their stylistic traits to other parts of the newspaper press and to television news media in general (Barnett and Gaber, 2001; Barnett, Seymour
and Gaber, 2000).

As the tabloid newspaper draws to a large extent on the patterns and
the traditions of working-class entertainment, it is an obvious source of
material for a wider range of products in a media world dominated by
popular entertainment values. It is more connected to everyday life and
tends to relegate the serious to a secondary place and foreground the
carnival and the colloquial (Conboy, 2006: 212). Carnival, for Bakhtin,
was: 'the suspension of all hierarchical rank, privileges, norms, and
prohibitions' (Bakhtin, 1984: 10) and represented the participation in
the overturning of orders of hierarchy by the common people themselves. Popular tabloid newspapers, and their generic offspring, are
able, at their most successful, to blend the attractiveness of these features of the culture of the ordinary people and their perceptions of a
utopian alternative to their daily existence and represent them as part
of their everyday lives. The strategic importance of the language of
these transactions is hard to underestimate. Bakhtin's 'carnivalesque' is
the temporary suspension of hierarchies of status, taste, behaviour,
while it allows a utopian glimpse of a community of plenty, freedom,
creativity. Its uncrownings and inversions, the transformations into a
new existence, unfettered by the exigencies of the everyday are, in the
tabloids, returned into a cycle which redirects these impulses back into
a circle of consumption and commodification. The transformations are
imagined via the reflected glories of celebrity, the uncrownings particularly of celebrities as politicians and sports stars are channelled into a
cycle of elevation and reduction. It is because the popular tabloids can

maintain and mutate this cultural mode of the carnivalesque that they retain their success although it is a triumph of genre over content in that it does not allow the radical contestations of social or economic hierarchies envisaged by Bakhtin's analysis to emerge. Throughout history, carnival has served to keep alive alternative conceptions of life and power relations. In the popular tabloids, we have a ventriloquized version of the freedom and laughter of Bakhtin's carnival table talk. It is a carnivalesque which only allows a limited perspective of individual and miraculous change (Langer, 1998) while mimicking its tone of transgression. Employing a carnivalesque mode explains how they retain an authority. They maintain the stance of the newspapers as on the side of common sense, against the powerful, on the side of the little man and woman even if, as media institutions, they belong to structures of the capitalist elite. They articulate that stance in the mocking, deflating language purloined from the common people's armoury.

The popular tabloids' version of dialogue is not, as in Bakhtin, opposed to the closure of the authoritarian word, nor is carnival opposed to the official hierarchy of culture, rather, their version is deployed as a strategy to envelop popular traditions within a rhetoric of laughter and ridicule but emptied of anything other than a hollow, ironic resistance to the all-pervasive nature of control.

Overall, the mockery, trivialization and conversationalization of the tabloid newspapers provide a pervasive sense of the 'carnivalesque' across the media which they permeate.

From a positive perspective, Docker claims that the carnivalesque keeps alive alternative conceptions of life and power relations (1994: 150). Although not a panacea it is, as in other rhetorical strategies within popular culture, a continuity in positioning the popular vis-à-vis the power elite while being encompassed by its constraints – popular culture as breathing space we might say.

Conclusion

It is the 'public idiom' (Hall, 1978) of these tabloid and tabloidized newspapers which links them so effectively to the everyday lives of their readers. In deploying this idiom with continuing commercial and cultural success, they play an important role in broader technological and social shifts in terms of news values and the popularization of public information. It is predominantly the selection of vocabulary, metaphorical associations, intertextual references to other popular media and echoes of colloquial discourse which places them so aggressively within the contemporary frame. As I have argued elsewhere, to understand contemporary British society we need to be familiar with the language of the tabloid agenda (Conboy, 2006 2007a).

The tabloids are a very distinctive version of what Halliday has called a 'social semiotic' (Halliday, 1978: 109). In using a range of distinctive and identifiable registers and dialects (Conboy, 2006), the tabloids enable the reader to use the newspaper as a textual bridge between their own experience of the culture in which they live, and their own attitudes and beliefs within a range of language which is a close approximation to what they imagine themselves to be using when they speak of these things themselves. In other words, the tabloids speak their language. Tabloids combine dialect and register in their deployment of a language which draws on social sensitivities about who uses which forms of language. In appropriating the language of the ordinary people of the country – the non-elite – the tabloids have managed to produce a marketable combination of social class and language. The language of the popular tabloids, even as it spreads to the elite press and other media formats, is a commercially astute attempt to construct what Bourdieu (1990) has called the *habitus* of its readership; a clever and profitable game of ventriloquism by the journalists and sub-editors with a clear appeal to the readers that it targets (Conboy, 2006: 12).

It is important to be able to assess the success of this style of language and not dismiss it in the way of the moral panic identified by Gripsrud (Gripsrud, 2000: 287). Its permeation into other media areas (Conboy, 2007a) is driven by changes in the acceptability of popular culture across the board and not just within the news media. This language is important not simply as a communicator of these social shifts but as a component of them at the same time. Tabloid language is not just about layout, it is not just about finding a new level of vulgarity and sensation. Its most important characteristic is the way in which it has extended the appeal of its core values and its cultural references, designed initially to appeal to a particular strand of blue-collar readership, to broader social groupings. It brings a patriotic consensus, a deep political scepticism, a tendency to view the world through the prism of celebrity and a sexualization to our everyday culture.

Contemporary newspapers across the board display the characteristics of the tabloid in either major or minor keys. The tabloid is a complex of attitudes, values, technology and economics but ultimately they have their ultimate expression in language. The language of the tabloids and its various manifestations as it crosses into mainstream media and other formats than the traditional popular tabloid newspaper is characterized by an extreme level of familiarity with its perceived audience; it is wired to contemporary trends and personalities in other forms of popular culture, notably television and film and makes frequent use of these intertextual references as points of identification with its audiences; is infused with slang and a vulgar vernacular; is highly sexualized in both its narratives and its semantics; is framed very much by a set of narratives which are nationalistically even chauvinistically based and is redolent of a culture which is sceptical or even dismissive of authority figures in society especially politicians. In turn, this language displays much of the ambivalent dynamism of contemporary culture. As in previous manifestations over 400 years, the language of newspapers is an excellent starting point for broader social exploration.

7 Technology and newspaper language: The reshaping of public communication

Introduction

Technologies of communication in the early twenty-first century allow a more rapid response and a livelier interaction with the views of newspaper readers. There is a clear market logic in the response of newspapers who are keen to incorporate letters, reader-driven features and User-Generated Content and to sharpen the specifics of their lifestyle appeal in order to maintain reader loyalty in an era of media fragmentation. A casualty of these processes has been the prime function of 'news' which appears to have been replaced in the contemporary newspapers by a range of views, lifestyle commentary and analysis appropriate to the various communities targeted by individual newspapers. All this has continued to shape the language of newspapers in their engagement with a reconfigured social setting. The relationship of this linguistic adaptation to broader social changes implicit in a period of rapid technological innovation will be the focus of this final chapter. These developments, however, emerge from a longer relationship between technology and newspapers and it is the shaping of these technologies historically which has determined to date the ways in which newspapers are responding to contemporary challenges to their style and content. The language which is undergoing such structural and stylistic changes today, for instance, is a relatively recent adaptation to the all-pervasive influence of the technology of the telegraph:

> The telegraph has been a crucial technological influence on news practices and forms, establishing the period in which news and news work assumed its modern pattern: a quest to get the story first, before one's competitors, and the use of a nonchronological format for writing stories. Technological developments in the pursuit of timeliness continue to impel news coverage towards 'present-ation' – that is, closing the gap between the event and its telling, with the goal of displaying events in 'real time'. (Bell, 1996: 3–4)

Technology and the language of the press

Throughout the history of the newspaper, technology has influenced its style and content. On occasions, technologies of transport and communication divorced from issues specifically related to the production of the newspaper have had an influence on the shaping of newspaper language just as significant as innovations in the production process itself. The *Daily Mail* from 1896 is a good example of this. Harmsworth introduced new technologies into the production process, developed national distribution on a scale and with an efficiency never previously seen and exploited new revenue from carefully targeted marketing. This meant that it incorporated much of the bite-size, carefully constructed boxes of information which had become so successful in magazine-style digests of news such as the pioneering *Tit-Bits* of Newnes (1881) ensuring shorter, more disparate pieces of news framed in shorter articles with clear headings. But, as always, these technological developments enhanced wider social and political trends. They allowed the newspaper to generate a volume of sales sufficient to cater to a lower middle class readership at an affordable price and ensured a product which was written and laid out in a way which would appeal simultaneously to this newly enfranchised readership and to the advertisers who subsidized it. The mass-market newspaper, in order to fit the information within the spaces between the plethora of advertisements, separated information from the style of language in which it arrived at the newspaper and related it in a concise and unadorned style (Matheson, 2000: 565). This process of internal editing not only harnessed technological and presentational changes, it also meant that the new readership could be addressed in a single style and tone of news more efficiently articulated than before. The launch of the *Daily Mail* was the key moment for the development on a mass daily basis of a vehicle which could effectively combine appeal to a new readership with all the technologies of mass production and distribution. This consolidated a much longer process which had seen the centrifugal spinning of the market between an elite press and a popular Sunday market.

This internally edited, truncated language was further formalized by the development of the inverted pyramid layout. This was not a technique driven solely by a technological appropriation of the telegraph which had been a reliable form of communication since the 1870s but, more typical of the impact of technology on newspapers throughout history, as a combination of commercial and technical responses to the need for newspapers to improve the communicative quality of their product (Pöttker, 2003: 509). It emigrated quickly from America to the

137

United Kingdom within the newly commercialized forces unleashed by Harmsworth's *Mail* and Pearson's *Express*. Targeting specific social classes of readers on behalf of advertisers, who could reasonably expect that their financial outlay was well directed, required the newspapers to shape the layout and the content of their product to the perceived lifestyles and interests of their readers. The inverted pyramid with its selective prioritizing of key facts in descending order of importance, therefore, had genuine social impact, meaning that 'the communicative quality of the texts improved considerably, making them more understandable' (Pöttker, 2003: 509).

The narrative chronological style characteristic of the late Victorian period gave way quickly to the new structure (Pöttker, 2003: 503). Even in the United States, Schudson observes the first examples in the 1880s and 1890s (Schudson, 1978: 61–87) but this was by no means the standard form by then. Within a relatively short period, however, it was swept in on the tide of radical reformulation of the mass dailies to the extent that by the 1920s the inverted pyramid had become the only form of reporting taught to journalists (Errico et al., 1997: 8).

The market-driven rationalization of the language of the new mass newspapers also affected the grammar of the reduced sentences which were increasingly identifiable as journalistic, meaning that '. . . markers of cause, effect and time adverbs are also usually lacking in news stories as opposed to more general narratives' (Bell, 1996: 12).

Beyond the mechanistic changes to the language of the newspapers which this innovation brought, Carey has argued that it has also had a profound yet often unacknowledged ideological impact:

> The telegraph also reworked the nature of written language and finally the nature of awareness itself . . . telegraphic journalism divorced news from an ideological context that could explain and give significance to events . . . By elevating objectivity and facticity into cardinal principles, the penny press abandoned explanation as a primary goal. (Carey, 1987)

Broadcasting: Action and reaction

The establishment of a carefully circumscribed and monitored set of communication styles through radio and later television broadcasting, although initially a challenge to newspapers, eventually led to their being able to develop a set of discourses quite at odds with those of broadcasting. The latter were mandated as purveyors of a public service to provide impartial and balanced approaches, especially to political news. The newspapers were able, like never before, to develop individual 'voices' which best articulated the views and styles of their readers and to deal more provocatively and in partisan fashion with the dominant political topics of the day. In the postwar era, it was clear that newspapers would have to shift their focus from the latest news, since radio could purvey this more reliably and quickly, and instead to consolidate their more opinionated and even sensationalist human-interest aspects.

The newsreels, popular in cinemas throughout the 1920s, had not been considered a serious source of rivalry by the newspaper owners, perhaps because of their weekly nature and the fact that viewers had to leave their homes to watch them, whereas radio journalism caused alarm among proprietors even in its initial experimental period. On the launch of the BBC in 1923, the Newspaper Proprietors' Association persuaded the government to prohibit news broadcasts before 7 p.m., so as not to damage sales of newspapers. The company was initially forced to rely on news supplied by outside agencies such as Reuters rather than developing its own newsgathering apparatus; concern about the potential political impact of this new medium (Smith, 1973: 22) also led to a ban on political commentary and controversy on the radio. Throughout the 1930s, however, newspapers were forced to react more creatively to the perceived threat posed by radio news to their circulations. As the immediacy of their news was becoming less of an imperative, they were obliged to concentrate more on commentary and opinion. This was accompanied, particularly in the popular newspapers, by a more visual approach to layout triggered by the revolutionary redesign of the *Daily Express* in 1933 with its better use of space, integration of illustration, bolder headlines and reader-friendly print (Conboy, 2002: 114–126).

Even though it took many years, well into World War II, for the BBC to be able to build up its own network of correspondents, by the end of the war it was the most trusted news medium for the majority of the British population. As well as the declining public trust in many newspapers which had insisted until relatively late in the day that there would be no war, including those who supported the fascists, Engel claims that the war was the turning point as people switched on their radios to hear the latest and most accurate news (1996: 141). Laconically, but with more than a pinch of truth, Tom Driberg argued that the main role of the BBC had been to teach people to stop believing newspapers – 'newspapers at any rate of the more garish sort' (Briggs, Vol. V, 1995: 69).

The rise in the reputation of radio journalism's reliability led to three shifts in the language of the newspapers. First, they had a justification to be more opinionated in contrast to the prohibition of editorializing on the BBC and its statutory obligation to maintain political balance.

Second, they began an incremental shift towards patterns of popular speech and a more 'rounded' view of the social experience and aspirations of readers. Third, they developed a more punning, less informational style of headline, with a diminishing need for the literal style of radio and later television. All of these trends were more noticeable first in the popular press but over the course of the next half-century had become identifiable across the board as part of the process of popularization (LeMahieu, 1988).

Newspapers continued to adapt their style to the further developments in broadcast journalism introduced through the medium of television journalism. These changes continued to be framed very much along the lines of the BBC's public service remit endorsed by a succession of government committees' reports (Sykes Report, 1923; Crawford Report, 1926; Ullswater Report, 1936; Beveridge Report, 1951). In fact, it was the greater trust placed in broadcasting as a medium for news because of this public service ethos, which ensured that as early as the 1950s, television had become the main source of news about the world for the general public. In 1955, the ITV introduced a commercially funded, much more populist, accessible and less deferential style of news coverage which had borrowed much from American practices and which prompted the press to take risks and push back boundaries in a bid to retain the allegiance of young readers (Bingham, 2004: 14). The mass popular press responded by aiming 'below television' (Tunstall, 1996: 59) with gossip and behind-the-scenes material as well as features and interviews and gossip on the stars whereas the elite press began experiments with a range of specializations aimed at the new professional classes, particularly in the public sector. Newspapers also exploited the new technological environment for their own purposes and developed an interesting codependence on television as it provided opportunities for previews and reviews of television programmes and also, particularly but not exclusively, in the popular press, a host of stories on the stars and commentary based on the storylines of popular television programmes. All newspapers began to employ media correspondents who maintained close links with this fertile territory for entertaining, profitable and easy news sources.

Despite improved printing and photographic technologies (the best example being *Picture Post* from 1938–1957 which provided photo-illustrated social reports and had a steady readership of over a million) and despite the improved visual layout and construction of stories in much of the press, World War II restricted any further development particularly in the daily press, because paper was in short supply. Post-war restrictions on paper, in fact, continued until 1955 and kept printing and paper costs low and advertising space at a premium. What did not change though were the extremely high production costs in what remained a labour-intensive industry. From the 1970s, technology had been available to reduce the dependency of newspapers on a volatile and disruptive workforce. The organization of print unions and journalist chapels ensured that the management remained locked into a labyrinth of archaic production practices. Proprietors and managers were aware of new printing systems that could have reduced manning. Print workers knew about them too, and were determined to retain their jobs by preventing the introduction of cost saving, or, in their terms, job-destroying technology (Greenslade, 2003: 245).

Once paper was back in plentiful supply, some things moved quickly while others continued to stagnate. The *Sunday Times* dominated the 1960s with its serializations and its Insight team of investigative journalists. The *Guardian* rose to prominence within a left-leaning culture of specialist writing for the expanding public sector professions such as education and social services. Advertising expansion also brought in extra pagination to allow for more analysis and commentary, particularly in these areas as the *Guardian* managed to tie advertising for jobs in these expanding employment areas with a need for more content dedicated to these new professions. One of the *Guardian's* strengths was its women's pages under the leadership of Mary Stott from 1957–1971 who pioneered feature writing that was a step forward from the agony aunts and problem pages of magazines and popular press in attempting to widen the resonance and reach of journalism aimed at women. As the world began to open up to women, she gave space to writing about balancing work and child-raising, depression, physical problems relating to women and she also included letters from readers who were allowed to play their part in opening up a new public sphere of women's discussion and engaged women of all classes, opening up the possibility of direct action and organization to effect change in their own lives and in the lives of other women (Chambers, Steiner and Fleming, 2004: 39). Other newspapers, especially the elite press, moved commercially to include more of interest to increasingly affluent and socially engaged professional women readers.

The trend towards naming individual journalists, particularly in the specialist columns, gathered momentum. More commentary, often depending on idiosyncratic opinion, meant that individual journalists' writing could hardly continue to be published without a byline. Television increasingly needed articulate commentators on the sorts of specialist subjects now covered in the papers which meant, in turn, that named journalists could enhance their reputation and that of their paper by appearing live on screen as expert contributors. The last bastion of anonymity was the *Times* which resisted until 1967. Another significant accelerant to the rise of the named specialist journalist was the figure of the newscaster, particularly on the ITN from 1955 and star interviewers such as David Frost and Robin Day, whose personal styles made up much of the appeal of television. Seymour-Ure has commented on the wider implications of the decline of anonymity:

> Anonymity, like the uniform of nurses or the police, highlights the role, not the person performing it. In journalism, it therefore bolstered the idea of objectivity in reporting the news. Its disappearance fitted an era in which electronic media were taking over the 'hot' news role and papers were selling the personal expertise of their staff at interpretation, comment, analysis, more than for traditional hard news. (Seymour-Ure, 1996: 155)

The Wapping Revolution

As 1896 had triggered the first mass newspapers, 1986 marked the beginning of a radically new era for newspapers and, albeit obliquely, for their language. Over one weekend, Rupert Murdoch moved the entire British newspaper production of his News International Company to a purpose-built site in the east end of London at Wapping. The building of the facility was no secret but no one could be sure of its purpose. He had suggested it was to provide a home for a new London evening paper, the *London Post* but this turned out to be nothing but a mischievous rumour. The plant was designed with security as a priority, predicting the political turmoil it would provoke as Murdoch refused the legitimacy of the printers' strike action and dismissed them without redundancy payment while persuading most of the journalists at astonishingly short notice to begin work at this new site, by crossing a hostile picket line. It was a prolonged and decisive struggle between Murdoch and the print unions and their allies but one which Murdoch won, altering the face of British newspapers as he did so. The events which began on 26 January 1986 were not termed the Wapping Revolution flippantly, as this was literally an overnight change in the organization of a whole industry despite the fact that, like most revolutions, it had been smouldering for a decade or so before it erupted. Rothermere caught the abruptness of this change when he claimed: 'There was before Wapping and there was after Wapping' (MacArthur, 1988: 106) and it has been correctly described as the 'decisive moment' in the history of the British press (Eldridge, Kitzinger and Williams, 1997: 37).

Yet Wapping's 'new' technologies were simply not that new. In 1973, the *Nottingham Evening Post* had become the first to experiment with technology which allowed journalists to directly input their copy.

The Royal Commission on the Press as early as 1977 had identified that the new technologies available even at that point would enable improved management and profitability of national newspapers. Technologically, Fleet Street was straggling behind. Reuters and the Stock Exchange were already using electronic transmission but the sudden shift to a modernized method of producing national newspapers would depend on political manoeuvring as much as technological innovation. By the mid-1980s, the technology benefited from a political climate which was extremely favourable to employers and a government which appeared to have customized anti-trades union legislation in order to smooth the profitable transition to new production practices on behalf of favoured newspaper owners.

Direct journalist-input without printers had been trialled by Eddie Shah's Messenger group of provincial newspapers in 1983 when he emerged victorious in his conflict with the NGA print union. The new journalist-input allowed for late corrections and updates to be included giving much more flexibility than before along with a much reduced wages bill. The 1984 Trade Union Act further eased the introduction of this technology. For instance, it restricted picketing to one's own place of work and limited the numbers entitled to picket. There could be no secondary action such as sympathy strikes in support of sacked or suspended workers and since Wapping was constituted as a separate company, any picketing by Murdoch's staff would be illegal. In addition, through the use of Australian road haulage company, Thomas Nationwide Transport, Murdoch also eliminated any interference by rail unions. Computer-based typesetting replaced the linotype production which had necessitated skilled and experienced printers and allowed for the immediate dismissal of 5,000 printers (Goodhart and Wintour, 1986: xi) which lowered costs, promised less interference in production, increased profits and quickly led to a more supine workforce of journalists on individual contracts.

Important though it is to set the political context, it is, however, the impact of these changes on the style and substance of newspapers post-Wapping which we need to concentrate on. It became much easier to produce additional sections and extra pagination as well as updating stories right up to deadline. Colour printing was also easier to incorporate. As a direct consequence of the Wapping Revolution, the 1990s saw trends accelerate towards more features, a 'big expansion in "non-news"' (Tunstall, 1996: 155).

Buoyant advertising markets assisted the extension of consumer journalism with less traditional news as a proportion of the paper and more sections on lifestyle, consumer issues and more cross-fertilization with other aspects of the entertainment industries, for example, sport, fashion and motoring. Post-1986 newspapers doubled or even trebled the number of their supplements and these sections contributed significantly to the identity of the papers and the image they wished to project to readers and of course advertisers.

The 'commentariat' has also grown as part of the heavyweight branding and identification of newspapers in an extremely competitive market. There has been an increase in the numbers of columnists of a variety of styles: polemical, analytical and satirical (McNair, 2008: 116). It is no surprise that Richard Littlejohn, as a columnist on the *Daily Mail*, is reputed to be the highest paid and therefore literally the most valued journalist in the country.

The *Independent*, founded in 1986, foregrounded photography and boasted the most complete arts and leisure listings of any national daily. The *Guardian* pioneered the second and third daily sections and especially its Tabloid G2. Yet it was the *Independent on Sunday* from 1990 which introduced innovations which were to materially accelerate many of these trends. It perfected a technique for heat-set colour printing on cheaper larger format paper which not only allowed more space for adverts but also allowed longer review material for journalists. The growth in supplements, length of review and shift towards a greater amount of consumer-driven, lifestyle journalism meant a proportionate reduction in old-style news and even in the traditional reporting style. This did not mean the disappearance of the inverted pyramid but certainly has contributed to its gradual marginalization within the totality of the newspaper.

A further significant observation in the post-Wapping newspaper concerns the politics of these newly expanded products. Despite increases in pagination and the growth of various styles of specialist features, Curran's research indicates that there remained 'significant difference . . . between a politicized elite press and a relatively depoliticized mass press' (Curran and Seaton, 2003: 93). Furthermore, the technological revolution did nothing to change the ideological range of the British press. It might have been heralded as a brave new technological era but it was structured by the old political economy. It reinforced a newspaper journalism led by commercialized consumer choice rather than one led by an altruistic vision of a contribution within a public sphere. The move to Wapping was a decisive political and technological step in that direction witnessing crucially: 'the decline of resources, manpower and time available for campaigning journalism' (Williams, 1998: 249).

This is a point which has been reinforced by more recent quantitative research as more pages filled by less full-time journalists. Lewis, Williams and Franklin (2008a 2008b) and Davies (2008) claim that contemporary journalists are driven by pressures of deadlines and profit margins to provide more copy in less time which draws uncritically on agency and PR material leaving less scope for independent, investigative journalism.

The online challenge: Impact and adaptation

The impact of the internet on the form and content of newspapers is as radical a change as this news medium has ever had to deal with and brings with it fundamental challenges to our social understanding of their function: 'Changes in form and distribution . . . change our concept of news' (Lewis, 2003: 96). This relationship to the social context of the web is inevitably having a related impact on the language and layout of newspapers. However, we still need to reaffirm the fact that communication history indicates that we should not be too quick to pen the obituary of the newspaper given the widespread evidence that 'The introduction of new media have rarely caused the elimination of existing media, although audiences and consequently their revenue bases do often shift' (Burnett and Marshall, 2003: 1). Newspapers need to adapt to this paradigm shift in mass communications and are already doing so, partially by incorporation of their product to an online format and partly by an adaptation of the printed product to the structures and capacity of the internet.

With the advent of the internet, the language as well as the layout and accessibility of the newspaper have begun to change out of all recognition. They have done this in part to retain readers but also to align themselves more to the apparent democratic imperatives of online interactivity. Boxes, annotations, sidebars, blogs, web-links, user generated content, responses to journalists' pieces in virtual debate, all contribute to changes not only in the newspapers but in their relationship with the readers as part of wider changes in the social nature of newspaper language. As well as it being progressively impossible to distinguish between online and paper versions of newspapers because of their inter-relatedness, there is a further impact on newspapers as they begin to import and adapt the layout and design features of their web-based versions in their printed columns; sidebars, topbars, breaking ticker tapes, references to hypertext and website material. The lack of closure in online news is impacting upon the length and structure of stories in printed form as it invites readers to cross-reference inside the newspaper and across formats to online links but, paradoxically it may seem, elsewhere in the commentary sections the newspaper is providing increased space for prolonged opinion and commentary pieces which would not fit onto a screen version in one viewing. This indicates how incorporation of online influences into the newspaper mainstream is taking place, at the same time as a further differentiation of the newspaper from its online and broadcast competitors/complements. This constitutes a complex re-engagement which is characteristic in its dynamics of the whole of newspaper history; dealing with alternative formats and changing technological demands as well as maintaining a language to socially engage with readership and community.

The way people are reading newspapers is changing fundamentally, fracturing the traditional audience-design model (Bell: 1984). They need to be much more dynamic and populist, using the new technological platform to provide a language which can couple the older idea of the mass with newer, more idiosyncratic appropriations as articulated in Negroponte (1995) and Lasica (2002):

> The interactive nature of the medium also demands new approaches and, for journalism, it has become clear that the tried and tested top-down forms, developed over the past three centuries around print, have been made obsolete by the new media and are increasingly irrelevant to the lives of many readers. (Hall, 2001: 2–3)

The online variant is having a flowback effect on the printed versions of newspapers. Newspapers in print currently try to accommodate the hyperlinks of cyberspace by providing printed hyperlink 'addresses', online contact details and e-mails as well as encouraging association with the broader 'brand' across to the online product itself. The compression and visualization of much of the material now presented in printed newspapers match the scannability of the shorter paragraphs, bulleted lists, news pegs and simple headlines of the online variety. In addition to presentation, journalism's content has responded, for instance, to the challenges posed by blogging by attempting to provide its own journalists' blog-responses within the online version of the newspaper. The extent to which this, by itself, will succeed is open to question. The tug-of-war between the ethical claims on public communication between bloggers and journalists (Singer, 2007) do not seem to have fundamentally shifted the ground of the debate since Bardoel reasserted the role of the journalist as 'broker of social consensus' (Bardoel 1996: 297). Indeed, the continuing primacy of mainstream journalism and journalists, especially newspaper journalists, as sources for online bloggers' own reports suggest, 'a more complementary relationship between weblogs and traditional journalism . . .' (Reese et al., 2007: 235). This relationship continues the trend for weblogs to reproduce as opposed to challenge the discourse of mainstream news media (Haas, 2005: 387) despite the fact that there is a plethora of alternative news media available (Atton, 2002) which could, in theory, destabilize the conventional hierarchies of topic and source provided by the mainstream media.

Boardman claims, however, that the differences are more fundamental than a shift of product or an imitation of certain stylistic elements implying that any short-term reconciliation between printed newspapers and online versions or any similarities between their modes of operation might be short-lived:

> The brain works by association and connection, and not in the linear way that the post-Gutenberg tradition of literacy requires of the reader.
>
> Hypertext is a way of hard-wiring these associations and connections with other documents – making permanent jumping-off points part of an electronic text . . . The hard-wired jumping-off points that take you to other documents are called hyperlinks. Written text allows us to replay the *content* of our experience and thought, but the revolutionary assumption behind hypertext is that we are replaying a narrative more like the *thought process* itself. (Boardman, 2005: 10)

Yet despite such claims that online news provides something dramatically novel in its 'non-linear' storytelling (Massey, 1), newspapers have rarely been read in a linear fashion and their structure and style seem complementary to online reading patterns rather than opposed to them. In addition, it seems clear that one prerequisite which online and hard copy newspaper will continue to share is a reliance on: '. . . traditional methods of careful and unbiased reporting, using compelling writing . . .' (Ward, 2002; Wilby, 2006; Barnett, 2008).

There are potentially democratic bonuses to these developments. For instance, in the first internet war, Lewis claims some of the benefits of online publication of news provided journalism with a greater range of involvement and dynamism:

> . . . it was not only regular journalists who reported on Kosovo, governmental agencies, international organizations. Local witnesses, freelance journalists, news agencies, academics and interested others all used the internet to publish news, background and comment on the crisis. (Lewis, 2003: 96)

Print newspapers are using features of the internet to enhance their appeal to readers, particularly a new generation of readers, providing what Pavlik claims might be 'a potentially better form of "contextualized" journalism' (Pavlik, 2001: xi). However, there are paradoxes at work in the democratic promise of online interactivity; on the one hand, the internet appears to flatten the hierarchy of traditional newspaper communication to readers while on the other the role of elite

147

commentators on the newspapers become highlighted and amplified as opinion brokers and gatekeepers to popular opinion through blogs and e-correspondence.

On the positive side, the elite press in particular have benefited from their ability to provide what is missing in instantaneous reporting; a reflective and analytical mode of commentary (continuing a trend from 1930s under the impact of another technological innovation) unavailable in most other news media although one increasingly framed by the values of the status quo. Furthermore, they have been able to offer spin-offs in the form of exhaustive web portals from their own archives to enable readers to pursue interests with increasing depth. Thus, elite newspapers become enablers, opening up from their own output into a range of parallel sources. The websites of national and local newspapers and interactive e-mail addresses of prominent columnists allow a more in-depth view of contemporary journalism while online archiving of stories and their links to related news sites is a boon for the engaged reader participant in the twenty-first century public sphere. This service is now opened up to more than the specialist researcher with huge potential for a broader and deeper perception of how events in the world are interlinked.

Conclusion

There are no easy or inevitable teleologies for newspaper language. They continue to exclude as much as include in their variants on public discourse. Up to the postwar era there was, according to Greenslade (2003: 628–629), very little directly targeted to a female audience. This has not changed to a large extent as Tuchman (1978) has identified in her withering assessment of the 'symbolic annihilation' of women in the quality press; to which we could add the almost complete 'sexualisation' (Holland, 1998) in the popular mass dailies.

Van Zoonen (1998) has observed that journalism is changing but within newspapers and their online variants, this change has merely provided more opportunities for the development of 'feminine' styles of writing in consumer-oriented and market-driven news such as human interest and emotional investment and the rise of the female confessional column (Heller, 1999):

> ... news is not inherently feminine or masculine. It is therefore not helpful to refer to the postmodern shift to infotainment as a 'feminization' of news . . . In the short run, however, femininity and so-called 'feminine news values' with an emphasis on human-interest stories are more marketable and are being exploited at the

> very moment when news is shifting as a genre from news to info-
> tainment. (Chambers, Steiner and Fleming, 2004: 230)

However, while we might agree thematically, there is significant evidence that 'real' news continues to remain stubbornly 'androcentric' (Simpson, 1993) and this can still be observed in the fabric of the newspaper's language today.

From the perspective of ethnic inclusivity, it is clear that elite racism, institutional racism and textual examples of everyday racism continue in contemporary newspaper journalism and continue to provide a significant obstacle to a more accurate social portrait of Britain in the twenty-first century. This is, however, hardly surprising when one considers the evidence of the Society of Editors' report *Diversity in the Newsroom* (2004) which demonstrates how a tiny proportion of journalists from ethnic minorities are employed on a range of local newspapers in areas with significant ethnic minority populations. This reinforces the point made by Van Dijk (1993) that within the newspaper industry there exists a patterning of selection of both news content and personnel, which is oriented towards a particular set of assumptions about the ethnic composition of the country. It is therefore no surprise that his research from 1991 has been endorsed by recent findings about the patterning of news about ethnic minorities in Britain in recent times (Richardson, 2004; Conboy, 2006, Greater London Authority, 2007; Runnymede, 2008).

The Sutton Trust's *The Educational Background of Leading Journalists* (2006) found a similar tale of under-representation of a wider social base, with independent schools and Oxford and Cambridge university background seemingly a distinct advantage in seeking advancement in the news media. National readership surveys indicate the extent to which newspaper readership is demarcated along social class lines while patterns of ownership and control have meant that a growing diversity of public representation has been severely stunted (Curran and Seaton, 2003: 102).

There has been much hypothesized about the future of the newspaper and other journalistic formats under the influence of technological developments such as the internet. They may be considered as part of a much longer debate on the impact of technology on journalism. As has been noted on many occasions, no mass medium has completely supplanted an existing one. The process of media development has always tended to be an additive one. The trends in new media influences on the contemporary newspaper seem to bear this out. The elite press have been quicker to develop cross-referenced archives with sophisticated website material while even popular tabloid newspapers seem to be

149

willing to complement the daily high street sale in an increasingly cut-throat market by an increasing web-presence.

Crystal sees the proliferation of English as the first truly global language and the related phenomenon of the language of the internet as two fronts of a revolutionary system. He sees the internet as being neither written nor spoken in its discourse but as a novel combination of the two; something *sui generis* and very much in formation at the present time (Crystal, 2004). This has interesting implications for the language of newspapers as they move online and as the internet has a flow-back influence on the content of newspapers in their continuing hard copy with a readership ever more used to online variants of news and other information and entertainment. Yet global English and the English of characteristically British newspapers continue to be different enough to confirm that newspapers continue to thrive because they can provide a cultural approximation of the specifics of time and place in their idiom and values. This is their attraction and the secret of their continuing success, not to be swallowed whole within a globalized, technological monolith but to find ways to retain what makes them relevant to specific audiences.

The traditional taxonomy of news values which include cultural proximity, socio-cultural values and consonance, will all continue to structure what particular communities want from their news and how it carries meaning for them. In many ways, the technological potential of the internet to provide a global, almost utopian model for news beyond traditional constraints may prove illusory. It is the socio-cultural specifics of the language of the news which determines the shape of the news itself. This is what needs to evolve if newspapers, in whatever form, are to continue to provide a forum for an increasingly diverse audience. No matter what the technological configuration, newspapers will sink or swim depending on the ways in which their language can capture and sustain a socially and culturally rooted audience.

Bibliography

Altschull, J.H. (1990), *From Milton to McLuhan: The Ideas Behind American Journalism*. London: Longman.

Anderson, B. (1986), *Imagined Communities*. London: Verso.

Andrews, A. (2000) [1859], *The History of British Journalism: From the Foundation of the Newspaper Press in England to the Repeal of the Stamp Act in 1855, with Sketches of Press Celebrities*. 2 Vols. London: Routledge/ Thoemmes.

Anon (1831), 'Useful knowledge'. *Westminster Review*. 7 (13) 14. April. 365–394.

Arnold, M. (1887), 'Up to Easter'. *The Nineteenth Century*, CXXIII, May. 627–648.

Atherton, I. (1999), 'The itch grown a disease: manuscript transmission of news in the seventeenth century' in J. Raymond (ed.), *News, Newspapers and Society in Early Modern Britain*. London: Frank Cass, pp. 39–65.

Atton, C. (2002), *Alternative Media*. London: Sage.

Atton, C. and Hamilton, J.F. (2008), *Alternative Journalism*. London: Sage.

Bakhtin, M.M. (1984), *Rabelais and His World* (trans. H. Iswolksky). Bloomington, IN: Indiana University Press.

Bakhtin, M.M. (1996), *The Dialogic Imagination*. M. Holquist (ed.), (trans. C. Emerson and M. Holquist). Austin, TX: University of Texas Press.

Baldasty, G.J. (1992), *The Commercialization of News in the Nineteenth Century*. Madison, WI: University of Wisconsin Press.

Bardoel, J. (1996), 'Beyond journalism: a profession between information society and civil society'. *European Journal of Communication*. 11 (3). 283–302.

Barnett, S. (2006), 'Reasons to be cheerful'. *British Journalism Review*. 17 (1). 7–14.

Barnett, S. (2008), 'On the road to self-destruction'. *British Journalism Review*. 19 (2). 5–13.

Barnett, S. and Gaber, I. (2001), *Westminster Tales: The Twenty-first Century Crisis in Political Journalism*. London: Continuum Press.

Barnett, S., Seymour, E. and Gaber, I. (2000), *From Callaghan to Kosovo: Changing Trends in British Television News*. Harrow: University of Westminster.

Baron, S. (2001), 'The guises of dissemination in early seventeenth century England: news in manuscript and print' in B. Dooley and S. Baron (eds), *The Politics of Information in Early Modern Europe*. London: Routledge, pp. 41–56.

Baylen, O. (1972), 'The "New Journalism" in late Victorian Britain'. *Australian Journal of Politics and History*. 367–385.

Baylen, O. (1979), 'The press and public opinion: W.T. Stead and the "New Journalism"'. *Journalism Studies Review*. 4. July. 45–49.

Beetham, M. (1996), *A Magazine of Her Own: Domesticity and Desire in the Women's Magazine 1800–1914*. London: Routledge.

Bell, A. (1984), 'Language style as audience design'. *Language in Society*. 13. 145–204.

Bell, A. (1991), 'Stylin' the news: audience design' in *The Language of the News Media*. Oxford: Blackwell, pp. 104–125.

Bell, A. (1996), 'Texts, time and technology in News English' in S. Goodman and D. Graddol (eds), *Redesigning English: New Texts, New Identities*. Milton Keynes: Open University Press, pp. 3–26.

Bell, M. (1997), 'TV news: how far should we go?'. *British Journalism Review*. 8 (1). 7–16.

Berridge, V. (1978), 'Popular Sunday papers and mid-Victorian society' in G. Boyce, J. Curran and P. Wingate (eds), *Newspaper History from the Seventeenth Century to the Present Day*. London: Constable, pp. 247–264.

Beveridge Report (1951), *Report of the Broadcasting Committee* [Cmnd 8116].

Billig, M. (1995), *Banal Nationalism*. London: Sage.

Bingham, A. (2004), *Gender, Modernity and the Popular Press in Inter-War Britain*. Oxford: Oxford University Press.

Bingham, A. (2009), *Family Newspapers: Sex, Private Life and the British Popular Press 1918–1978*. Oxford: Oxford University Press.

Bingham, A. and Conboy, M. (2009), 'The *Daily Mirror* and the creation of a commercial popular language: a people's war and a people's paper?'. *Journalism Studies*. 10 (5). 639–654.

Black, J. (1991), *The English Press in the Eighteenth Century*. Aldershot: Gregg Revivals.

Black, J. (2001), *The English Press 1622–1855*. Stroud: Sutton Publishing.

Black, S. (2008), 'The *Spectator* in the History of the Novel'. *Media History*. 14 (3). 337–352.

Blumenfeld, R.D. (1944), *The Press in My Time*. London. Rich and Cowan.

Boardman, M. (2005), *The Language of Websites*. London: Routledge.

Boston, R. (1990), *The Essential Fleet Street: Its History and Influence*. London: Blandford.

Bourdieu, P. (1990), *The Logic of Practice*. Cambridge: Polity Press.

Bourdieu, P. (1998), *On Television and Journalism*. London: Pluto.

Boyce, G. (1978), 'The Fourth Estate: the reappraisal of a concept' in G. Boyce, J. Curran and P. Wingate (eds), *Newspaper History from the Seventeenth Century to the Present Day*. London: Constable, pp. 19–40.

Brake, L. (1994), *Subjugated Knowledges: Journalism, Gender and Literature in the Nineteenth Century*. London: Macmillan.

Brake, L. (1988), 'The Old Journalism and the New: forms of cultural production in London in the 1880s' J.H. Wiener (ed.), *Papers for the Millions: The New Journalism in Britain, 1850s to 1914*. New York: Greenwood Press, pp. 1–24.

Brathwaite, R. (1631), *Whimzies: Or a New Cast of Characters*. London.

Brice, A.W. and Fielding, K.J. (1981), 'A New Article by Dickens: "Demoralisation and Total Abstinence"'. *Dickens Studies Annual*. 9. 1–19.

Briggs, A. and Burke, P. (2002), *A Social History of the Media: From Gutenberg to the Internet*. Cambridge: Polity Press.

Briggs, A. (1995), *The History of Broadcasting in the United Kingdom: Vol. V- Competition*. Oxford: Oxford University Press.

Bromley, M. (1998), 'The "tabloiding of Britain": "quality" newspapers in the 1990s' in H. Stephenson and M. Bromley (eds), *Sex, Lies and Democracy*. Harlow: Longman. pp. 24–38.

Bromley, M. and Tumber, H. (1997), 'From Fleet Street to cyberspace: the British 'popular' press in the late twentieth century'. *European Journal of European Communication Studies*. 22 (3). 365–378.

Brooks, P. (1984), *The Melodramatic Imagination*. New York: Columbia University Press.

Brown, L. (1985), *Victorian News and Newspapers*. Oxford: Clarendon Press.

Burnett, R. and Marshall, P.D. (2003), *Web Theory*. London: Routledge.

Burnham, E. (1955), *Peterborough Court: The Story of the Daily Telegraph*. London: Cassell and Company Ltd.

Calhoun, C. (1982), *The Question of Class Struggle: Social Foundations of Popular Radicalism During the Industrial Revolution*. Oxford. Basil Blackwell.

Cameron, D. (1990), Demythologizing sociolinguistics: why language does not reflect society' in J.E. Joseph and J.T. Talbot (eds), *Ideologies of Language*. London: Routledge. pp. 79–96.

Cameron, D. (1995), *Verbal Hygiene*. London: Routledge.

Cameron, D. (1996), 'Style policy and style politics: a neglected aspect of the language of the news'. *Media, Culture and Society*. 18. 315–333.

Campbell, K. (2000), 'Journalistic discourses and constructions of modern knowledge' in L. Brake, B. Bell and D. Finkelstein (eds), *Nineteenth Century Media and the Construction of Identities*. Basingstoke: Palgrave, pp. 40–53.

Campbell, K. (2001), 'Introduction: on perceptions of journalism' in K. Campbell (ed.), *Journalism Literature and Modernity: From Hazlitt to Modernism*. Edinburgh: Edinburgh University Press, pp. 1–14.

Capp, B. (1979), *Astrology and the Popular Press: English Almanacs 1500–1800*. London: Faber and Faber.

Carey, J.W. (1987), 'Why and how? The dark continent of American journalism' in R.K. Manoof and M. Schudson (eds), *Reading the News*. New York: Pantheon, pp. 162–166.

Carey, J. (1989), *Communication as Culture: Essays on Media and Society*. Boston, MA: Hyman Publishers.

Chalaby, J.K. (1998), *The Invention of Journalism*. Basingstoke: Macmillan.

Chambers, D., Steiner, L. and Fleming, C. (2004), *Women and Journalism*. London: Routledge.

Chippendale, P. and Horrie, C. (1992), *Stick It Up Your Punter: The Rise and Fall of the Sun*. London: Mandarin.

Christiansen, A. (1961), *Headlines All My Life*. London: Harper Row.

Clarke, B. (2004), *From Grub Street to Fleet Street: An Illustrated History of English Newspapers to 1899*. Aldershot: Ashgate.

Clegg, C.S. (1997), *Press Censorship in Elizabethan England*. Cambridge: Cambridge University Press.

Conboy, M. (2002), *The Press and Popular Culture*. London: Sage.

Conboy, M. (2003), 'Parochializing the global: language and the British tabloid press' in J. Aitchison and D. Lewis (eds), *New Media Language*. London: Routledge, pp. 45–54.

Conboy, M. (2004), *Journalism: A Critical History*. London: Sage.

Conboy, M. (2006), *Tabloid Britain: Constructing a Community through Language*. London: Routledge.

Conboy, M. (2006), 'Expanding Ethical Discourse in Wooler's *Black Dwarf*. *Ethical Space: The International Journal of Communication Ethics*. 2 (1). 13–19.

Conboy, M. (2007a), *The Language of the News*. London: Routledge.

Conboy, M. (2007b), 'Permeation and profusion: popular journalism in the new millennium'. *Journalism Studies*. 8 (1). 1–12.

Coward, R. (2007), 'What the butler started: relations between British tabloids and monarchy in the fall-out from the Burrell trial'. *Journalism Practice*. 1 (2). 245–260.

Crawford Report (1926), *Report of the Broadcasting Committee* [Cmnd 2599].

Crouthamel, J.L. (1989), *Bennett's New Herald and the Rise of the Popular Press*. Syracuse, New York: Syracuse University Press.

Crowley, T. (1990), 'That obscure object of desire: a science of language' in J.E. Joseph and J.T. Talbot (eds), *Ideologies of Language*. London: Routledge, pp. 27–50.

Crystal, D. (1991), *Dictionary of Linguistics and Phonetics*. Oxford: Basil Blackwell.

Crystal, D. (2004), *The Language Revolution*. Oxford: Polity Press..

Cudlipp, H. (1953), *Publish and Be Damned*. London: Andrew Dakers.

Cunningham, F. (1816) (ed.), *The Works of Ben Jonson*. 2 Vols. London: John Camden Hotten.

Curran, J. (1978), 'The press as an agency of social control: an historical perspective' in G. Boyce, J. Curran and P. Wingate (eds), *Newspaper History from the Seventeenth Century to the Present Day*. London: Constable, pp. 51–78.

Curran, J. (2002), 'Media and the making of British society c1700–2000'. *Media History*. 8 (2). 135–154.

Curran, J. and Seaton, J. (2003), *Power without Responsibility: The Press, Broadcasting and New Media in Britain*. London: Routledge.

Cust, R. (1986), 'News and politics in seventeenth century England'. *Past and Present*. 112. 60–90.

Dahlgren, P. (1988), 'What's the meaning of this? Viewers' plural sense-making of TV news'. *Media, Culture and Society*. 10. 285–301.

Darnton, R. (1996), *Forbidden Fruit*. New York: Harper Collins.

Dark, S. (1922), *The Life of Sir Arthur Pearson*. London: Hodder and Stoughton, p. 20.

154

Davies, N. (2008), *Flat Earth News*. London: Chatto and Windus.

De Cilla, R., Riesigl, M. and Wodak, R. (1999), 'The discursive construction of national identities'. *Discourse and Society*. 10 (2). 149–173.

De Burgh, H. (2000), *Investigative Journalism*. London: Routledge.

de Saussure, F. (1966), *Course in General Linguistics* (trans. W. Baskin). New York: McGraw Hill.

Deuze, M. (2005), 'Popular journalism and professional ideology: tabloid reporters and editors speak out'. *Media, Culture and Society*. 27 (6). 861–882.

Docker, J. (1994), *Postmodernism and Popular Culture*. Cambridge: Cambridge University Press.

Douglas, G.H. (1999), *The Golden Age of the Newspaper*. Westport, CT: Greenwood Press.

Dyck, I. (1992), *William Cobbett and Rural Popular Culture*. Cambridge: Cambridge University Press.

Eagleton, T. (1991), *The Function of Criticism: From the Spectator to Post-Structuralism*. London: Verso.

Edelman, M. (1966), *The Mirror: A Political History*. London: Hamish Hamilton Ltd.

Edwards, P.D. (1997), *Dickens's 'Young Men': George Augustus Sala, Edmund Yates and the World of Victorian Journalism*. Ashgate: Aldershot.

Eldridge, J., Kitzinger, J. and Williams, K. (1997), *The Mass Media and Power in Modern Britain*. Oxford: Oxford University Press.

Eley, G. (1992), 'Nations, publics, and political cultures: placing Habermas in the nineteenth century' in C. Calhoun (ed.), *Habermas and the Public Sphere*. Cambridge, MA: MIT Press, pp. 289–339.

Elliott, P. (1978), 'Professional ideology and organisational change: the journalist since 1800' in G. Boyce, J. Curran and P. Wingate (eds), *Newspaper History from the Seventeenth Century to the Present Day*. London: Constable, pp. 172–191.

Emery, M. and Emery, E. (1992), *The Press and America: An Introspective History of the Mass Media*. Englewood Cliffs, NJ: Prentice Hall.

Engel, M. (1996), *Tickle the Public: One hundred years of the popular press*. London: Gollancz and Prentice Hall.

Ensor, R. (1968), *The Oxford History of England: Vol. XIV: 1870–1914*. Oxford: Oxford University Press.

Entmann, R.M. (1993), 'Framing: toward clarification of a fractured paradigm'. *Journal of Communication*. 43 (4). 51–58.

Epstein, J. (1976), 'Fergus O'Connor and the *Northern Star*'. *International Review of Social History*. 21. 51–97.

Errico, M., April, J., Asch, A., Khalfani, L., Smith, M. and Ybarra, X. (1997), 'The evolution of the Summary News Lead' in *Media Monographs*. I (1). www.scripps.ohiou.edu/mediahistory/mhmjour1-1.htm

Erskine-Hill, H. and Storey, G. (eds) (1983), *Revolutionary Prose of the English Civil War*. Cambridge: Cambridge University Press.

Evans, H. (1972), *Editing and Design. Volume One: Newsman's English*. London: Heinemann.

Fairclough, N. (1995a), *Critical Discourse Analysis*. London: Routledge.

Fairclough, N. (1995b), *Media Discourse*. London: Routledge.

Fairclough, N. (2003), *Analysing Discourse: Textual Analysis for Social Research*. London: Routledge.

Fairclough, N. (2005), *Analyzing Discourse: Textual Analysis for Social Research*. Abingdon, Oxon: Routeldge.

Fairlie, H. (1957), 'Brilliance skin-deep'. *Encounter*. July. 8–14.

Foucault, M. (1974), *The Archaeology of Knowledge* (trans. A.M. Sheridan). London: Tavistock.

Fowler, J. (1991), Language in the News: Discourse and Ideology and in Press. Routledge: London.

Fox-Bourne, H.R. (1998), *English Newspapers*. Vols. 1 and 2. London: Thommes/Routledge.

Frank, J. (1961), *The Beginnings of the English Newspaper*. Cambridge, MA: Harvard University Press.

Franklin, B. (1997), *Newszak and News Media*. London: Arnold.

Franklin, B. (2004), *Packaging Politics: Political Communication in Britain's Media Democracy*. London: Arnold.

Friedman, J. (1993), *Miracles and the Pulp Press During the English Revolution*. London: University College Press.

Friederichs, H. (1911), *The Life of Sir George Newnes*. London: Stodder and Houghton.

Frost, C. (2007), *Journalism Ethics and Regulation*. London: Longman.

Gilmartin, K. (1996), *Print Politics: The Press and Radical Opposition in Early Nineteenth Century England*. Cambridge: Cambridge University Press.

Goldsworthy, S. (2006), 'English non-conformity and the pioneering of the modern newspaper campaign'. *Journalism Studies*. 7 (3). 387–402.

Goodbody, J. (1985), 'The *Star*: its role in the rise of popular newspapers 1888–1914'. *Journal of Newspaper and Periodical History*. 1 (2). 20–29.

Goodhart and Wintour (1986), *Eddie Shah and the Newspaper Revolution*. Sevenoaks, Kent: Coronet Books.

Graves, R. and Hodge, A. (1971), *The Long Weekened: A Social History of Britain 1918–1939*. Harmondsworth: Penguin.

Greater London Authority (2007), 'The search for common ground Muslims, non-Muslims and the UK media: a report commissioned by the Mayor of London' http://www.london.gov.uk/mayor/equalities/docs/commonground _report.pdf

Greenslade, R. (2003), *Press Gang: How Newspapers Make Profits From Propaganda*. Basingstoke: Macmillan.

Gripsrud, J. (2000), 'Tabloidization, popular journalism and democracy' in C. Sparks and J. Tulloch (eds), *Tabloid Tales*. Oxford: Rowman and Littlefield, pp. 285–300.

Haas, T. (2005), 'From "Public Journalism" to the "Public's Journalism"? Rhetoric and reality in the discourse on weblogs'. *Journalism Studies*. 6 (3). 387–396.

Haas, T. (2007), The Pursuit of Public Journalism: Theory, Practice and Criticism. London: Routledge.

Habermas, J. (1992), *The Structural Transformation of the Public Sphere*. Cambridge: Polity Press.

Hall, S. (1978), 'The social production of news' in S. Hall, C. Critcher, T. Jefferson, J. Clarke and B. Roberts (eds), *Policing the Crisis: Mugging, The State and Law and Order*. London: Macmillan, pp. 55–57.

Hall, J. (2001), *Online Journalism: A Critical Primer*. London: Pluto Press.

Halliday, M.A.K. (1978), Language as Social Semiotic: The Social Interpretation of Language and Meaning. London: Arnold.

Hampton, M. (2001), '"Understanding media": theories of the press in Britain, 1850–1914'. *Media, Culture and Society*. 23 (2). 213–231.

Hampton, M. (2004), *Visions of the Press in Britain, 1850–1950*. Urbana and Chicago, IL: University of Illinois Press.

Harcup, T. (2006), *The Ethical Journalist*. London: Sage.

Harcup, T. and O'Neill, D. (2001), 'Galtung and Ruge revisited'. *Journalism Studies*. 2 (2). 261–280.

Harris, B. (1996), *Politics and the Rise of the Press: Britain and France 1620–1800*. London: Routledge.

Harris, R. (1980), *The Language Makers*. London: Duckworth.

Harrison, S. (1974), *Poor Men's Guardians*. London: Lawrence and Wishart.

Heller, Z. (1999), 'Girl Columns' in S. Glover (ed.), *Secrets of the Press: Journalists on Journalism*. Harmondsworth: Penguin, pp. 10–17.

Helsinger, E.K. (1997), 'Cobbett's Radical Husbandry', *Rural Scenes and National Representation: Britain 1815–1850*. Princeton, NJ: Princeton University Press, pp. 103–140.

Hendrix, R. (1976), 'Popular humour in the Black Dwarf'. *Journal of British Studies*. 16. 108–128.

Hodge, R. and Kress, G. (1993), *Language as Ideology*. London: Routledge.

Hoggart, R. (1958), *The Uses of Literacy*. Harmondsworth, Middlesex: Pelican.

Holland, P. (1983), 'The page 3 girl speaks to women too'. *Screen*. 24 (3). 84–102.

Holland, P. (1998), 'The politics of the smile: "Soft news" and the sexualization of the Popular Press' in C. Carter, G. Branston and S. Allen (eds), *News, Gender and Power*. London: Routledge, pp. 17–32.

Hollis, P. (1970), *The Pauper Press*. Oxford: Oxford University Press.

Hughes, C. (1986), 'Imperialism, illustration and the *Daily Mail* 1896–1904' in M. Harris and A.J. Lee (eds), *The Press in English Society from the Seventeenth to the Nineteenth century*. London and Toronto: Associated University Presses, pp. 187–200.

Humpherys, A. (1990), 'Popular narrative and political discourse in *Reynolds's Weekly Newspaper*' in L. Brake, A. Jones and L. Madden (eds), *Investigating Victorian Journalism*. Basingstoke: Macmillan, pp. 32–46.

Hunt, L. (1998), *British Low Culture: From Safari Suits to Sexploitation*. London: Rotledge.

Jackson, K. (2000), 'George Newnes and the "loyal tit-bitites" – editorial identity and textual interaction in *Tit-Bits*' in L. Brake, B. Bell and D. Finkelstein (eds), *Nineteenth Century Media and the Construction of Identities*. Basingstoke: Palgrave, pp. 11–26.

Jackson, K. (2001), *George Newnes and the New Journalism in Britain, 1880–1910 Culture and Profit*. Aldershot: Ashgate.

157

Jäger, S. (2001), 'Discourse and knowledge: theoretical and methodological aspects of a critical discourse and dispositive analysis' in R. Wodak and M. Meyer (eds), *Methods of Critical Discourse Analysis*. London: Sage, pp. 32–62.

James, L. (1976), *Print and the People*. London: Allan Lane.

Johnson, S. and Ensslin, A. (2007), *Language and the Media*. London: Continuum.

Jones, A. (1996), *Powers of the Press: Newspapers, Power and the Public in Nineteenth Century England*. Aldershot: Ashgate, Scolar Press.

Jones, S. (1997), 'The *Black Dwarf* as Satiric Performance; or, the instabilities of the "Public Square"' in S.C. Behrendt (ed.), *Radicalism, Romanticism and the Press*. Detroit, MI: Wayne State University Press.

Joseph, J.E. and Taylor, T.J. (eds) (1990), *Ideologies of Language*. London: Routledge.

Jucker, A.H. (2005), 'News discourse: mass media communication from the seventeenth to the twenty-first century' in J. Skaffari, M. Peikola, R. Carroll, R. Hiltunen and B. Wårvik (eds), *Opening Windows on Texts and Discourses of the Past*. Amsterdam/Philadelphia, PA: John Benjamins, pp. 7–21.

Juergens, G. (1966), *Joseph Pulitzer and the New York World*. Princeton. NJ: Princeton University Press.

Klancher, J.P. (1987), *The Making of English Reading Audiences 1790–1832*. Madison, WI: University of Wisconsin Press.

Knelman, J. (1992), 'Subtly sensational: a study of early Victorian crime reporting'. *Journal of Newspaper and Periodical History*. 8 (1). 34–41.

Koss, S. (1981 and 1984), *The Rise and Fall of the Political Press in Britain*. 2 vols. Chapel Hill, NC: University of North Carolina Press.

Laclau, E. and Mouffe, C. (1985), *Hegemony and Socialist Strategy*. London: Verso.

Langer, J. (1998), *Tabloid Television: Popular Journalism and the 'Other News'*. London: Routledge.

Lasica, J. (2002), 'The promise of the Daily Me'. *Online Journalism Review*. www.ojr.org/ojr/lasica/1017779142.php

Lee, A.J. (1976), *The Origins of the Popular Press 1855–1914*. London: Croom Helm.

LeMahieu, D.L. (1988), *A Culture for Democracy: Mass Communication and the Cultivated Mind in Britain Between the Wars*. Oxford: Clarendon.

Levy, F. (1999), 'The decorum of news' in J. Raymond (ed.), *News, Newspapers and Society in Early Modern Britain*. London: Frank Cass, pp. 12–38.

Lewis, D. (2003), 'Online news: a new genre?' in J. Aitchison and D. Lewis (eds), *New Media Language*. London: Routledge, pp. 95–104.

Lewis, J., Williams, A. and Franklin, B. (2008a), 'A compromised fourth estate?' *Journalism Studies*. 9 (1). 1–20.

Lewis, J., Williams, A. and Franklin, B. (2008b), 'Four rumours and an explanation: a political economic account of journalists' changing newsgathering and reporting practices'. *Journalism Practice*. 2 (1). 27–45.

Locke, D. (1980), *A Fantasy of Reason: The Life and Thought of William Godwin*. London: Routledge and Kegan Paul.

158

MacArthur (1988), *Eddy Shah, Today and the Newspaper Revolution*. London: David and Charles.

Maccoby, S. (1955), *English Radicalism: 1786–1832 from Paine to Cobbett*. London: Allen and Unwin.

MacManus, (1995), *Market-Driven Journalism: Let the Citizen Beware*. London: Sage.

Marr, A. (2005), *My Trade: A Short History of British Journalism*. London: Pan Macmillan.

Massey, B.L. (2004), 'Examination of 38 Web Newspapers Show Non-Linear Storytelling'. *Newspaper Research Journal*. 25 (3). 96–102.

Matheson, D. (2000), 'The birth of news discourse: changes in news language in British newspapers, 1880–1930'. *Media, Culture and Society*. 22 (5). 557–573.

McCalman, I. (1998), *Radical Underworld: Prophets, Revolutionaries, and Pornographers in London, 1795–1840*. Cambridge: Cambridge University Press.

McDowell, P. (1998), *The Women of Grub Street*. Oxford: Oxford University Press.

McGuigan, J. (1993), *Cultural Populism*. London: Routledge.

McLachlan, S. and Golding, P. (2000), 'Tabloidization in the British press: a quantative investigation into changes in British newspaper' in C. Sparks and J. Tulloch (eds), *Tabloid Tales*. Oxford: Rowman and Littlefield, pp. 75–90.

McNair, B. (2003), *An Introduction to Political Communication*. London: Routledge.

McNair, B. (2008), 'I, Columnist' in B. Franklin (ed.), *Pulling Newspapers Apart*. London: Routledge, pp. 112–120.

Mendle, M. (2001), 'News and the pamphlet culture of mid-seventeenth century England' in B. Dolley and S. Baron (eds), *The Politics of Information in Early Modern Europe*. London: Routledge, pp. 57–79.

Mill, S. (1989), *'On Liberty' and Other Writings*. S. Collini (ed.). Cambridge: Cambridge University Press.

Miller, C.R. (1994), 'Rhetorical community: the cultural basis of genre' in A. Freedman and P. Medway (eds), *Genre and the New Rhetoric*. London: Routledge, pp. 67–79.

Montgomery, M. (2007), *The Discourse of Broadcast News: A Linguistic Approach*. London: Routledge.

Mott, F.L. (1962), *American Journalism: A History of Newspapers in the US Through 250 Years*. Basingstoke: Macmillan.

Negrine, R. (1994), *Politics and the Mass Media in Britain*. London: Routledge.

Negroponte, N. (1995), *Being Digital*. New York: Vintage Books.

Nerone, J.C. (1987), 'The mythology of the penny press'. *Critical Studies in Mass Communication*. 4. 376–404.

Nordin, K.D. (1979), 'The entertaining press: sensationalism in eighteenth century Boston newspapers'. *Communication Research*. 6 (3). 295–320.

O' Connell, S. (1999), *The Popular Print in England*. London: The British Museum Press.

O'Connor, T.P. (1889), 'The new journalism'. *New Review*. 1. October. 423–434.

O'Neill, D. and O'Connor, C. (2008), 'The passive journalist: how sources dominate local news'. *Journalism Practice.* 2 (3). 487–500.

Ong, W. (1982), *Orality and Literacy: The Technologizing of the Word.* London: Methuen.

Palmer, M. B. (1983), *Des Petits Journaux aux Grandes Agences: naissance du journalisme moderne.* Aubier-Montaigne: Paris.

Pavlik, J.V. (2001), *Journalism and the New Media.* New York: Columbia University Press.

Pennycook, A. (2004), 'Performativity and language studies'. *Critical Inquiry in Language Studies: An International Journal.* 1 (1). 1–19.

Pincus, S. (1995), '"Coffee politicians does create": Coffeehouses and restoration political culture'. *The Journal of Modern History.* 67 (4). 807–834.

Pocock, J.G.A. Schochet, G.J. and Schwoerer, L.G. (eds) (1993), *The Varieties of British Political Thought.* Cambridge: Cambridge University Press.

Pöttker, H. (2003), 'News and its communicative quality: the inverted pyramid – when and why did it appear?' *Journalism Studies.* 4 (4). 501–511.

Pugh, M. (1998), 'The *Daily Mirror* and the revival of labour'. *Twentieth Century British History.* 9 (3). 420–438.

Raymond, J. (1996), *The Invention of the Newspaper: English Newsbooks, 1641–1649.* Oxford: Oxford University Press.

Raymond, J. (ed.) (1999), *News, Newspapers and Society in Early Modern Britain.* London: Frank Cass.

Read, D. (1961), *Press and the People, 1790–1850.* London: Edward Arnold.

Reese, S., Rutigliano, L., Kidewk, H. and Jeong, J. (2007), 'Mapping the blogosphere: citizen-based media in the global news era'. *Journalism: Theory, Practice, Criticism.* 8 (3). 235–262.

Reeve, H. (1855), 'The newspaper press'. *Edinburgh Review.* Cii, October. 470–498.

Rhoufari, M.M. (2000), 'Talking about the tabloids: journalists' views' in C. Sparks and J. Tulloch (eds), *Tabloid Tales.* Oxford: Rowman and Littlefield, pp. 163–176.

Richardson, J.E. (2004), *(Mis)Representing Islam: The Racism and Rhetoric of the British Broadsheet Press.* Amsterdam: John Benjamins.

Richardson, J.E. (2007), *Analyzing Newspapers: An Approach from Critical Discourse Analysis.* Basingstoke: Palgrave Macmillan.

Robson (1995), *Marriage or Celibacy? The Daily Telegraph on a Victorian Dilemma.* Toronto: University of Toronto Press.

Rooney, D. (2000), 'Thirty years of competition in the British tabloid press: the *Mirror* and the *Sun* 1968–1998' in C. Sparks and J. Tulloch (eds), *Tabloid Tales.* Oxford: Rowman and Littlefield, pp. 91–110.

Runnymede Trust (April 2008), *A Tale of Two Englands: 'Race' and Violent Crime in the Press'.* Runnymede Trust, London. www.runnymedetrust. org/.../race-and-violent-crime-in-the-press.html

Rusbridger, A. (2005), 'The Hugo Young Memorial Lecture'. University of Sheffield. 9 March.

Said, E. (1978), 'The problem of textuality: two exemplary positions'. *Critical Enquiry.* 4. 673–714.

Schiller, D. (1981), *Objectivity: The Public and the Rise of Commercial Journalism*. Philadelphia, PA: University of Pennsylvania Press.

Schudson, M. (1978), *Discovering the News: A Social History of American Newspapers*. New York: Harper.

Schudson, M. (2008), 'Public spheres, imagined communities, and the underdeveloped historical understanding of journalism' in B. Zelizer (ed.), *Explorations in Communication and History*. Abingdon, Oxon: Routledge, pp. 181–189.

Schults, R. (1972), *Crusader in Babylon: W.T. Stead and the Pall Mall Gazette*. Lincoln, NE: University of Nebraska Press.

Scollon, R. (1998), *Mediated Discourse as Social Interaction: A Study of News Discourse*. London: Longman.

Seymour-Ure, C. (1996), *The British Press and Broadcasting Since 1945*. Oxford: Blackwell.

Seymour-Ure, C. (2000), 'Northcliffe's legacy' in P. Caterall, C. Seymour-Ure and A. Smith (eds), *Northcliffe's Legacy*. Basingstoke: Macmillan, pp. 9–25.

Sherman, S. (2001), 'Eyes and ears, news and plays: the argument of Ben Jonson's *Staple*' in B. Dooley and S.A Baron (eds), *The Politics of Information in Early Modern Europe*. London: Routledge, pp. 23–39. Siebert, F.S. (1965), *Freedom of the Press in England, 1476–1776: The Rise and Fall of Government Control*. Urbana, IL: Urbana University Press.

Simpson, P. (1993), *Language, Ideology and Point of View*. London: Routledge.

Singer, J.B. (2007), 'Contested autonomy: professional and popular claims on journalistic norms'. *Journalism Studies*. 8 (1). 79–95.

Skerpan, E. (1992), *The Rhetoric of Politics in the English Revolution*. Columbia, MS: University of Missouri Press.

Slater, M. (1997), *Dickens' Journalism: 'The Amusements of the People' and Other Essays, Reports and Reviews 1834–51*. London: Dent.

Smith, A.C. (1973), *The Shadow in the Cave*. London: Allen and Unwin.

Smith, A.C. (1975), *Paper Voices*. London: Chatto & Windus.

Smith, A.C. (1978), 'The press and popular culture: an historical perspective' in G. Boyce, J. Curran and P. Wingate (eds), *Newspaper History from the Seventeenth Century to the Present Day*. London: Constable, pp. 41–50.

Smith, O. (1984), *The Politics of Language 1719–1819*. Oxford: Clarendon.

Snoddy, R. (1992), *The Good, The Bad and The Unacceptable*. London: Faber.

Society of Editors (2004), *Diversity in the Newsroom*. London: Society of Editors.

Sommerville, J. (1996), *The News Revolution*. Oxford: Oxford University Press.

Sparks, C. (2000), 'Introduction: the panic over tabloid news' in C. Sparks and J. Tulloch (eds), *Tabloid Tales*. Oxford: Rowman and Littlefield, pp. 1–40.

Sparks, C. and Tulloch, J. (eds) (2000), *Tabloid Tales*. Oxford: Rowman and Littlefield.

Stead, W.T. (1886), 'The future of journalism'. *Contemporary Review*. 50. November. 663–679.

Stevens, J. (1991), *Sensationalism and the New York Press*. New York: Columbia University Press.

Sutton Trust (2006), *The Educational Background of Leading Journalists*, London: Sutton Trust.

Swales, J. (1990), *Genre Analysis*. Cambridge: Cambridge University Press.

Sykes Report (1923), *Broadcasting Committee: Report* [Cmnd 1951].

Taylor, A.J.P. (1976), *English History 1914–1945*. Oxford: Clarendon.

Taylor, T.J. (1990), 'Which is to be master' in J.E. Joseph and J.T. Talbot (eds), *Ideologies of Language*. London: Routledge, pp. 9–26.

Taylor, S.J. (1992), *Shock! Horror! The Tabloids in Action*. London: Black Swan.

Thomas, J. (2005), *Popular Newspapers, The Labour Party and British Politics*. London: Routledge.

Thompson, E.P. (1967), *The Making of the English Working Class*. London: Penguin.

Tuchman, G. (1978), 'The symbolic annihilation of women by the mass media' in G. Tuchman, A. Kaplan Daniels and J. Benet (eds), *Hearth and Home: Images of Women in the Mass Media*. New York: Oxford University Press, pp. 3–45

Tulloch, J. (2007), 'Charles Dickens and the voices of journalism' in R. Keeble and S. Wheeler (eds), *The Journalistic Imagination: Literary Journalists from Defoe to Capote and Carter*. Abingdon, Oxon: Routledge, pp. 58–73.

Tunstall, J. (1996), *Newspaper Power: The New National Press in Britain*. Oxford: Clarendon.

Ullswater Report (1936), *Report of the Broadcasting Committee* [Cmnd 5091].

Van der Weyde, W.M. (1925), *The Life and Works of Thomas Paine: Volume VI The Rights of Man*. New Rochelle, NY: Thomas Paine National Historical Association.

Van Dijk, T. (1991), *Racism and the Press*. London: Sage.

Van Dijk, T. (1993), *Elite Discourse and Racism*. London: Sage.

Van Leeuwen, T. (1987), 'Generic strategies in press journalism'. *Australian Review of Applied Linguistics*. 10 (2). 199–220.

Van Zoonen, L. (1998), '"One of the girls": the changing gender of journalism' in C. Carter, G. Branston and S. Allan (eds), *News, Gender and Power*. London: Routledge, pp. 33–46.

Vincent, D. (1993), *Literacy and Popular Culture*. Cambridge: Cambridge University Press.

Voss, P.J. (2001), *Elizabethan News Pamphlets*. Pittsburgh, PA: Dusquesne University Press.

Walker, A. (2006), 'The development of the provincial press in England 1780–1914'. *Journalism Studies*. 7 (3). 373–386.

Ward, M. (2002), *Journalism Online*. Oxford: Focal press.

Watt, T. (1991), *Cheap Print and Popular Piety, 1550–1640*. Cambridge: Cambridge University Press.

Wickwar, W.H. (1928), *The Struggle for the Freedom of the Press*. London: George Allen and Unwin Ltd.

Wiener, J. (ed.) (1985), *Innovators and Preachers: The Role of the Editor in Victorian England*. Westport, CT: Greenwood Press.

Wiener, J. (ed.) (1988), *Papers for the Millions: The New Journalism in Britain, 1850–1914*. New York: Greenwood Press.

Wiener, J. (1996), 'The Americanization of the British press' in M. Harris and T. O'Malley (eds), *Studies in Newspaper and Periodical History: 1994 Annual*. Westport, CT: Greenwood Press, pp. 61–74.

Wiener, J. and Hampton, M. (eds) (2007), *Anglo-American Media Interactions, 1850–2000*. Basingstoke: Palgrave Macmillan.

Wilby, P. (2006), 'Brave new world?'. *British Journalism Review*. 17 (4). 15–21.

Williams, F. (1957), *Dangerous Estate*. Harlow: Longman Green.

Williams, K. (1998), *Get Me A Murder a Day: A History of Mass Communication in Britain*. London: Arnold.

Williams, R. (1961), *The Long Revolution*. Harmondsworth: Penguin.

Williams, R. (1976), *Keywords: A Vocabulary of Culture and Society* London: Fontana, Croom Helm.

Williams, R. (1978), 'The press and popular culture: an historical perspective' in G. Boyce, J. Curran and P. Wingate (eds), *Newspaper History from the Seventeenth Century to the Present Day*. London: Constable, pp. 41–50.

Wiseman, S.J. (1999), 'Pamphlet plays in the civil war news market: genre, politics and "context"' in J. Raymond (ed.), *News, Newspapers and Society in Early Modern Britain*. London: Frank Cass, pp. 66–83.

Wodak, R. (2001), 'The discourse-historical approach' in R. Wodak and M. Meyer (eds), *Methods of Critical Discourse Analysis*. London: Sage, pp. 63–94.

Wood, M. (1994), Radical Satire and Print Culture 1790–1822. Oxford: Clarendon Press.

Woolf, D. (2001), 'News, history and the construction of the present in early modern England' in B. Dooley and S. Baron (eds), *The Politics of Information in Early Modern Europe*. London: Routledge, pp. 80–118.

Zagorin, P. (1969), *Court and Country: The Beginnings of the English Revolution*. London: Routledge.

Index